SpringerBriefs in Education

W0036885

We are delighted to announce SpringerBriefs in Education, an innovative product type that combines elements of both journals and books. Briefs present concise summaries of cutting-edge research and practical applications in education. Featuring compact volumes of 50 to 125 pages, the SpringerBriefs in Education allow authors to present their ideas and readers to absorb them with a minimal time investment. Briefs are published as part of Springer's eBook Collection. In addition, Briefs are available for individual print and electronic purchase.

SpringerBriefs in Education cover a broad range of educational fields such as: Science Education, Higher Education, Educational Psychology, Assessment & Evaluation, Language Education, Mathematics Education, Educational Technology, Medical Education and Educational Policy.

SpringerBriefs typically offer an outlet for:

- An introduction to a (sub)field in education summarizing and giving an overview of theories, issues, core concepts and/or key literature in a particular field
- A timely report of state-of-the art analytical techniques and instruments in the field of educational research
- A presentation of core educational concepts
- An overview of a testing and evaluation method
- A snapshot of a hot or emerging topic or policy change
- An in-depth case study
- A literature review
- A report/review study of a survey
- An elaborated thesis

Both solicited and unsolicited manuscripts are considered for publication in the SpringerBriefs in Education series. Potential authors are warmly invited to complete and submit the Briefs Author Proposal form. All projects will be submitted to editorial review by editorial advisors.

SpringerBriefs are characterized by expedited production schedules with the aim for publication 8 to 12 weeks after acceptance and fast, global electronic dissemination through our online platform SpringerLink. The standard concise author contracts guarantee that:

- an individual ISBN is assigned to each manuscript
- each manuscript is copyrighted in the name of the author
- the author retains the right to post the pre-publication version on his/her website or that of his/her institution

More information about this series at http://www.springer.com/series/8914

Jack Frawley · Tran Nguyen · Emma Sarian
Editors

Transforming Lives and Systems

Cultural Competence and the Higher Education Interface

OPEN ACCESS

Editors
Jack Frawley
National Centre for Cultural Competence
The University of Sydney
Sydney, NSW, Australia

Tran Nguyen
National Centre for Cultural Competence
The University of Sydney
Sydney, NSW, Australia

Emma Sarian
National Centre for Cultural Competence
The University of Sydney
Sydney, NSW, Australia

ISSN 2211-1921   ISSN 2211-193X   (electronic)
SpringerBriefs in Education
ISBN 978-981-15-5350-9   ISBN 978-981-15-5351-6   (eBook)
https://doi.org/10.1007/978-981-15-5351-6

This Springer imprint is published by the registered company Springer Nature Singapore Pte Ltd.
The registered company address is: 152 Beach Road, #21-01/04 Gateway East, Singapore 189721,
Singapore

Acknowledgements

The editors and authors acknowledge and pay respect to the traditional custodians of the lands where Australian universities now stand, and the contribution they make to higher education. The editors wish to thank the many contributors to this book, including the authors and peer-reviewers, the staff of the National Centre for Cultural Competence.

Contents

1 The National Centre for Cultural Competence: Transformative
  Journeys   1
  Jack Frawley, Tran Nguyen, and Emma Sarian

2 Creating Effective Cultural Competence Workshops
  for Australian Higher Education Staff   9
  Amy McHugh-Cole, Rachael Simons, and Gabrielle Russell

3 Methodology for Evaluating the University of Sydney's
  Culturally Competent Leadership Program 21
  Alessandra Pecci, Jack Frawley, and Tran Nguyen

4 Deconstructing and Embedding Cultural Competence in Initial
  Teacher Education: Responding to University Graduate
  Qualities for Undergraduate Students 39
  Sheelagh Daniels-Mayes

5 Navigating the Cultural Interface to Develop a Model for Dentistry
  Education: Cultural Competence Curricula in Dentistry
  Education 51
  Cathryn Forsyth, Stephanie D. Short, Michelle Irving, Marc Tennant,
  and John Gilroy

6 Fostering Diversity Competence in the Veterinary Curriculum 63
  Jaime Gongora, Meg Vost, Sanaa Zaki, Stewart Sutherland,
  and Rosanne Taylor

7 Progressing STEM Education Using Adaptive, Responsive
  Techniques to Support and Motivate Students 75
  Collin Grant Phillips and Fu Ken Ly

Contents

Chapter 1
The National Centre for Cultural Competence: Transformative Journeys

Jack Frawley, Tran Nguyen, and Emma Sarian

Abstract The University of Sydney's National Centre for Cultural Competence (NCCC) hosts professional development programmes for professional staff and academics to be able to actively, ethically, respectfully and successfully engage in intercultural settings, including the ability to engage meaningfully with cultures, histories and contemporary issues of Aboriginal and Torres Strait Islander communities. In addition, several resources and online modules have been developed for students. These programmes and resources support staff and students from across the University to develop their capability, capacity and resilience for cultural competence and help deepen connections between leadership, cultural competence and Aboriginal and Torres Strait Islander contexts. It is suggested in this chapter that transformative learning is best suited to cultural competence education.

Keywords Cultural competence · Transformative learning · Cultural change

Introduction

In the planning phase for establishment of the National Centre for Cultural Competence (NCCC) it was foreseen that it would be the first knowledge centre in Australia specifically established to foster scholarship and research in and translation of cultural competence. Over the six years of the funding period, the NCCC would evolve into a nationally and internationally recognised leader in the development of cultural competence knowledge and practice. The programmes and activities of the NCCC would align with and be informed by the University of Sydney's *Wingara Mura—Bunga Barrabugu Aboriginal and Torres Strait Islander Integrated Strategy* (University of Sydney, 2012). The *Wingara Mura* strategy sets out a whole-of-university approach to the development and integration of Indigenous cultures, pedagogies and epistemologies within the University, including the establishment of cultural competence as a graduate quality.

J. Frawley (✉) · T. Nguyen · E. Sarian
National Centre for Cultural Competence, The University of Sydney, Sydney, NSW, Australia
e-mail: jack.frawley@sydney.edu.au

© The Author(s) 2020
J. Frawley et al. (eds.), *Transforming Lives and Systems*,
SpringerBriefs in Education, https://doi.org/10.1007/978-981-15-5351-6_1

The strategic vision of the NCCC was not only that it would inform, shape and promote cultural competence narratives, action and capability to the university community at the first instance, but also widen its reach both nationally and internationally. While initially focused on, and built on an Australian Indigenous foundation, the NCCC would increase its relevance to other diverse communities, especially within the University of Sydney context, and contribute to the development of the university as culturally competent and in doing so contribute to the professional development of its staff and the academic success of its students.

Cultural competence has been described as an evasive concept to define, and that the emphasis instead should be on viewing the concept as a transformative journey. The interdisciplinary field is also scattered with other interrelated concepts such as cultural humility, cultural responsiveness, cultural plasticity, intercultural competence and multicultural competence. Even so, it is the definition of cultural competence by Cross et al. (1989) that has the most traction. Cross et al. (1989, p. iv) define cultural competence as 'a set of congruent behaviours, attitudes, and policies that come together in a system, agency, or among professionals and enables that system, agency, or those professionals to work effectively in cross-cultural situations'. Cross et al. (1989) emphasise that a culturally competent system should value diversity and have the capacity for individuals and systems to be able to undertake cultural self-assessment. The University of Sydney's 2016–2020 strategy views cultural competence as a key quality in addressing excellence as well as a discrete graduate quality, that is embedded as a learning outcome in every degree. The NCCC, while still in its early stages, has been instrumental in supporting a whole-of-university approach to the strategic plan, policies and programmes that assist academic and professional staff and students to navigate their journey through a cultural competence landscape, and these transformative journeys including perspectives on practice and projects are described in this volume.

The Cultural Competence and Higher Education Interface: The National Centre for Cultural Competence Foundational Work

Cultural competence has increasingly been viewed as a necessary response to growing diversity in higher education in Australia and other countries. Specifically, cultural competence is considered as one of the important tools that higher education institutions can use to respond to globalisation (Palmer & Carter, 2014). It is also a channel through which the academy expresses its voice for social justice (Sherwood & Russell-Mundine, 2017; Kruse, Rakha, & Calderone, 2018). In parallel with developing students' cultural competence (Goodman, 2013), there have also been similar calls to programmes and initiatives promoting cultural competence for staff. Some key aims of this novel professional development approach are to enable staff in higher education to adapt well to the diversifying workforce, to work effectively with diverse populations and being responsible for teaching in such a way that demonstrates a commitment to the principle of respect for all (Brown, 2004).

Cultural change in higher education, as Kruse and colleagues (2018) have acknowledged, is neither easy nor certain. The authors observe that it is not that higher education institutions have not strived to enable staff and students to become culturally competent, but that they have performed this in uncoordinated and unsystematic ways. Sherwood and Russell-Mundine (2017) when discussing the NCCC's effort of promoting cultural competence within the University of Sydney context also recognise that one of the greatest challenges for the Centre is to be strategic about where it should focus its efforts. Furthermore, it is important for each higher education institution to determine the desired outcomes of cultural competence that it aims to achieve, either cognitive, attributional, experiential and/or behavioural at both individual and institutional level, the latter with a focus on policy and practice (Bezrukova, Jehn, & Spell, 2012).

There have also been significant barriers and challenges to the development of cultural competence at the higher education interface. For example, people with long-held beliefs may resist a strong behavioural change-oriented programme focused on understanding specific areas of difference (Bezrukova et al., 2012). Staff may also raise significant questions about what cultural competence actually means, why it is important, what intercultural skills and knowledge should students acquire in a globalised world and what roles academics and institutions play in mentoring students in developing cultural competence (Pinto, 2018). Additionally, the dominant neo-liberalist environment in higher education today can hinder the development of a cultural competence agenda when this project may have to compete with other agendas and goals (Kruse et al., 2018).

Reviewing the current literature, Kruse and colleagues (2018) identify six conditions that they contend are necessary to support strong cultural competence agendas in higher education. These conditions include:

1. *Time to meet, learn and process new learning*—with the focus on allowing staff to have the opportunity to interact and work with people, as well as on staff's knowledge development;
2. *Time to monitor, evaluate and refine processes and practices across the campus*—this will enable higher education institutions to evaluate their progress in achieving the desired outcomes of cultural competence;
3. *Communication structures that support the work of cultural competence*—those structures can include different forms, for example, both face-to-face or online communication that foster the exchange of ideas, discussion and networking within and across the institution;
4. *A climate of trust and openness to improvement and learning*—with trust expressed in various forms such as institution members' willingness to participate in events and dialogue;

5. *Supportive leadership* from higher education institutions such as presidents, provosts, deans or department chairs—such leadership is critical to determine whether or not cultural competence agendas are to be successful;
6. *Access to expertise designed to support individual and organisational learning,* as the attainment of cultural competence requires faculty and staff to have access to expertise in content and practice.

At the University of Sydney, the establishment of the NCCC is viewed as a critical starting point to develop a whole-of-institution agenda of cultural competence on campus. The NCCC's work over the past five years since its inception illustrates the Centre's efforts to lay important foundations for cultural change to take place at the University. With the ultimate aim of instigating cultural competence as a transformational change and social justice education agent (Sherwood & Russell-Mundine, 2017), the NCCC has increasingly expanded its research and teaching work both within and beyond the University campus. The NCCC has developed foundational resources to support and encourage University staff to take up cultural competence philosophy and pedagogy in their curriculum, teaching and research.

One of the NCCC's key activities is delivering workshops that focus on foundational elements of cultural competence such as developing critical self-reflection capabilities, understanding socialisation and worldview, or understanding one's cultural identities (see Sherwood & Russell-Mundine, 2017; McHugh-Cole, Simons and Russell this volume). Additionally, through its Culturally Competent Leadership Program (CCLP) (see Pecci, Frawley and Nguyen this volume), the NCCC has created a valuable and exciting opportunity for University staff to have time to meet, network and exchange ideas about promoting cultural competence on campus and beyond.

The NCCC's other significant work includes the development of online learning modules which have facilitated greater access for both University staff and students to gain better knowledge about cultural competence (National Centre for Cultural Competence, 2019). In 2018, the NCCC hosted the international conference on *Cultural Competence and the Higher Education Sector: Dilemmas, Policies and Practice* (The University of Sydney, 2018). The conference created an important platform for academics and policy-makers to network, share information and create a national dialogue on the topic of cultural competence. The conference also provided an opportunity to explore different and innovative approaches and strategies that incorporate Indigenous knowledges and practices into the development and implementation of cultural competence in the higher education sector. The NCCC's work so far has thus contributed to producing a climate of trust and openness at the University that is essential to foster cultural competence, as well as building leadership capacity in the field. In recognition of the need to move beyond knowledge and skill acquisition, most cultural competence education programmes like those offered by the NCCC employ some form of transformative learning.

Transformative Practice and Perspectives

One of the overarching themes of the chapters in this book is the recognition that the pedagogy of cultural competence cannot be reduced to simple frameworks of knowledge or skill transfer. It is for this reason that many cultural competence educators have adopted, either implicitly or explicitly, the pedagogical framework of transformative learning. Introduced by Mezirow in 1978, transformative learning suggests that adult learning is a distinct process from childhood learning, and that traditional forms of instructivist pedagogy, in which information is passively delivered and consumed, is not a suitable or effective model for adult learners (Kitchenham, 2008).

Instead, Mezirow proposes that learning for adults should be understood in terms of 'perspective transformation', in which existing meaning-making frameworks are challenged by new information. Importantly, according to Mezirow, experiencing such a challenge is not enough on its own but requires critical self-reflection on the part of the learner, both to become aware of their existing frame and then to understand how new information challenges this frame. Thus, for Mezirow, perspective transformation is 'the emancipatory process of becoming critically aware of how and why the structure of psycho-cultural assumptions has come to constrain the way we see ourselves and our relationships, reconstituting this structure to permit a more inclusive and discriminating integration of experience and acting upon these new understandings' (Mezirow, 1981, p. 6).

It is for this reason that much of the literature on cultural competence has turned to the framework of transformative learning in order to think through pedagogical best practice, since it works from a conceptualisation of learning as self-directed and self-reflexive. A number of cultural competence educators point to the transformative learning framework as particularly suitable for developing cultural competence because it 'invokes having openness to the views and experiences of others, willingness to consider different beliefs and perspectives, listening with empathy, suspending hasty judgement and understanding the experiences that have shaped the views we hold' (Jackson, Power, Sherwood, & Geia, 2013, p. 107; see also Lewis, Lewis, & Williams, 2014; Taylor, 1994). While the transformative learning framework is not always explicitly acknowledged, its influence on the pedagogical practices explored within this book is clear.

In particular, four fundamental components of transformative learning have been identified by Taylor (2000) as integral to the development of cultural competence. These components are:

1. Group setting
2. Shared experiential learning
3. Value-laden content
4. Affective learning.

First, there is general consensus that cultural competence is best developed in a group setting, which reflects the transformative learning principle that learning requires listening to others and self-reflecting in order to evaluate what is being communicated (Mezirow, 2003). By facilitating cultural competence development within a group, cultural competence skills can immediately be engaged, as learners are exposed to worldviews that differ from their own within an environment that facilitates self-reflection on these differences. For instance, in Chap. 2, Cole et al. explore a model of cultural competence development that includes both online resources as well as face-to-face workshops, acknowledging the need for more traditional forms of knowledge transfer as well as facilitated group interaction.

Supplementary to this is a need for shared experiential learning, which can be defined as 'the process whereby knowledge is created through the transformation of experience' (Kolb, 2014, p. 38). This emphasis on experiential learning underscores how both transformative learning and cultural competence frameworks conceptualise meaning-making not exclusively as an intellectual process. In these terms, meaning-making frameworks are challenged by reflecting on experience, and this includes both prior lived experience as well as experiential learning activities. In Chap. 5, Forsyth et al. detail what this experiential self-reflection looks like in the process of integrating cultural competence within dentistry education, demonstrating that practising cultural competence is essential not only for students but also the staff who seek to include it within their curricula.

The third component for cultural competence development is value-laden content; that is, learning content must explicitly identify and encourage reflection on personal values, and how these align with the values of critical cultural competence education. In particular, the relationship between cultural competence and issues of inequality, power and social justice must be made clear in order to more explicitly challenge learners' worldviews. As Rivera (2010) suggest:

> the inconsistency between universally-espoused values of fairness and respect, on the one hand, and, on the other, prejudice and discrimination... can be explored in the classroom, with the expectation of dissonance and subsequent movement toward at least attempts at a resolution of value conflicts (2010, pp. 17–18; see also McGregor, 1993).

Both Daniels-Mayes and Gongora et al. raise these issues on embedding cultural competence within their curricula in Chaps. 4 and 6, respectively, and both of their programmes include student awareness of the social justice element in cultural competence as a key outcome.

Finally, the affective component of cultural competence learning must be engaged, in recognition of the relationship between emotional responses and how they invoke or impede self-reflection. In these terms, perspective transformation is not simply an intellectual process but also an emotional one, an element that was missing from Mezirow's initial model of transformative learning and which he later corrected (2000). Instead, as Taylor suggests, 'it is the learners' emotions and feelings that not only provide the impetus for them to reflect critically, but often provide the gist on which to reflect deeply' (Taylor, 2000, p. 16). In Chap. 7, Phillips and Ly consider the emotional dimension of maths education and the trauma that is sometimes associated with it, and the need for creating culturally safe spaces for students to regain their confidence.

Ultimately, as the chapters in this book demonstrate, it is this transformative aspect of cultural competence development that produces difficulties for integration into institutional systems such as the university. Questions around assessment, evaluation and metrics—foundational to the logics of contemporary university governance—are inevitably raised with the adoption of a transformative learning approach, and it is perhaps in this area that consistent evaluation of the University's current cultural competence policies and programmes is required. Nevertheless, the existing scholarship on critical cultural competence is clear that teaching cultural competence cannot and should not be reduced to a box-ticking exercise, and each of the experiences outlined in this book can be understood as responding to this tension in various ways.

Conclusion

The growing diversity in culture, knowledge, skills and capabilities that students bring to tertiary education requires appropriate pedagogical responses. Cultural competence education of both students and staff is viewed as an essential and appropriate tool in addressing diversity. Nevertheless, there is a corresponding need to move beyond knowledge and skills acquisition, to a more transformative experience underlined by learning that is self-directive and self-reflexive. Taylor's (2000) components of group setting, shared experiential learning, value-laden content and affective learning are viewed as being the key to developing cultural competence for both students and staff. At the University of Sydney, the NCCC to date has had a crucial and successful role in supporting staff and students to undertake their own transformative cultural competence journey.

References

Bezrukova, K., Jehn, K., & Spell, C. (2012). Reviewing diversity training: Where we have been and where we should go. *Academy of Management Learning and Education, 11*(2), 207–227.

Brown, L. (2004). Diversity: The challenge for higher education. *Race Ethnicity and Education, 7*(1), 21–34.

Cross, T. L., Bazron, B. J., Dennis, K. W., & Isaacs, M. R. (1989). Towards a culturally competent system of care: A monograph on effective services for minority children who are severely emotionally disturbed. Washington, DC: Child and Adolescent Service System Program Technical Assistance Center, Georgetown University Child Development Center.

Goodman, D. (2013). Cultural competency for social justice. Retrieved from https://acpacsje.wordpress.com/2013/02/05/cultural-competency-for-social-justice-by-diane-j-goodman-ed-d/.

Jackson, D., Power, T., Sherwood, J., & Geia, L. (2013). Amazingly resilient Indigenous people! Using transformative learning to facilitate positive student engagement with sensitive material. *Contemporary Nurse, 46*, 105–112. https://doi.org/10.5172/conu.2013.46.1.105.

Kitchenham, A. (2008). The evolution of John Mezirow's transformative learning theory. *Journal of Transformative Education, 6*, 104–123. https://doi.org/10.1177/1541344608322678.

Kolb, D. A. (2014). *Experiential learning: Experience as the source of learning and development.* FT Press.

Kruse, S. D., Rakha, S., & Calderone, S. (2018). Developing cultural competency in higher education: an agenda for practice. *Teaching in Higher Education, 23*(6), 733–750.

Lewis, P. H., Lewis, A. N., & Williams, F. D. (2014). Cultural competency in public administration programs. *Cultural Competency for Public Administrators, 244.*

McGregor, J. (1993). Effectiveness of role playing and anti-racist teaching in reducing student prejudice. *The Journal of Educational Research, 86,* 215–226. https://doi.org/10.1080/00220671. 1993.9941833.

Mezirow, J. (2003). Transformative learning as discourse. *Journal of Transformative Education, 1,* 58–63. https://doi.org/10.1177/1541344603252172.

Mezirow, J. (1981). A critical theory of adult learning and education. *Adult Education, 32,* 3–24. https://doi.org/10.1177/074171368103200101.

National Centre for Cultural Competence (2019). Learning Resources. Retrieved from https:// sydney.edu.au/nccc/training-and-resources/resources.html.

Palmer, J., & Carter, J. (2014). Working in the border zone: developing cultural competence in higher education for a globalised world. *Knowledge Cultures, 2*(4), 22–44.

Pinto, S. (2018). Intercultural competence in higher education: academics' perspectives. *On the Horizon, 26*(2), 137–147.

Rivera, M. A. (2010). The ethics of pedagogical innovation in diversity and cultural competency education. *The Innovation Journal, 15*(2), 1–18

Sherwood, J., & Russell-Mundine, G. (2017) How we do business: Setting the agenda for cultural competence at the University of Sydney. In J. Frawley, S. Larkin, & J. A. Smith J. (Eds), *Indigenous Pathways, Transitions and Participation in Higher Education.* Singapore: Springer Open.

Taylor, E. (2000). Fostering Mezirow's transformative learning theory in the adult education classroom: A critical review. *Canadian Journal for the Study of Adult Education, 14*(2), 1–28.

Taylor, E. W. (1994). Intercultural competency: A transformative learning process. *Adult Education Quarterly, 44,* 154–174. https://doi.org/10.1177/074171369404400303.

The University of Sydney. (2018). What role does cultural competence have in higher education? Retrieved from https://sydney.edu.au/news-opinion/news/2018/03/26/what-role-does-cultural-competence-have-in-higher-education–.html.

The University of Sydney. (2016). If you change nothing, nothing will change: 2016–2020 Strategic plan. Retrieved from https://www.sydney.edu.au/content/dam/intranet/documents/strategy-and-planning/strategic-plan-2016-20.pdf.

Chapter 2
Creating Effective Cultural Competence Workshops for Australian Higher Education Staff

Amy McHugh-Cole, Rachael Simons, and Gabrielle Russell

Abstract Cultural competence, and Indigenous cultural competence in particular, is recognised as a priority in Australian higher education (Universities Australia, 2011). There is a need to develop the knowledge, skills and attitudes required to engage respectively and effectively in Aboriginal and Torres Strait Islander contexts in tertiary education settings across the country (Universities Australia, 2011). This chapter details a study conducted by the National Centre for Cultural Competence (NCCC), in its journey to embed cultural competence across a large higher education workforce. The study documents the creation and delivery of in-person workshops to determine the effectiveness of this approach in building understandings of, and commitment to, cultural competence among staff.

Keywords Cultural competence · Higher education · Aboriginal and torres strait islander · Pedagogy · Curriculum · Workshop facilitation

Introduction

In 2014, the National Centre for Cultural Competence (NCCC) was established at the University of Sydney. The focus of the NCCC is to lead the thinking on and practice of cultural competence in line with the University's Strategic Plan (The University of Sydney, 2016). Staff and students' capacity to work in a culturally competent manner is an organisational priority of the University (The University of Sydney, 2016). The Strategic Plan aligns with the seminal model put forward by Cross et al. (1989, p. 7), which positions cultural competence as a 'set of congruent behaviours, attitudes, and policies that come together in a system, agency, or amongst professionals and enables that system, agency, or those professionals to work effectively in cross-cultural situations.' Kirmayer (2012) advocates that developing cultural competence at the organisational level and through the training and education of individual staff members is most effective. Cultural competence at the University is addressed at the strategic level, while the NCCC provides resources for University staff to develop

A. McHugh-Cole (✉) · R. Simons · G. Russell
National Centre for Cultural Competence, The University of Sydney, Sydney, NSW, Australia
e-mail: amy.cole@sydney.edu.au

© The Author(s) 2020 9
J. Frawley et al. (eds.), *Transforming Lives and Systems*,
SpringerBriefs in Education, https://doi.org/10.1007/978-981-15-5351-6_2

their cultural competence capabilities at the individual level. This paper explores the journey taken by the NCCC to create and deliver those cultural competence workshops for staff.

The NCCC privileges Aboriginal and Torres Strait Islander knowledges, histories and contemporary realities when engaging University staff on the cultural competence journey. This aligns with the view of Universities Australia (2011, p. 17) that positions universities as agents of change, not only in improving higher education experiences and attainment for Indigenous Australians within universities but also by making 'a commitment to the capacity building of Indigenous communities' to reach more equitable outcomes for access and participation within these institutions.

In addition to prioritising Aboriginal and Torres Strait Islander contexts, the NCCC seeks to support and celebrate diversity at the University. The Australian Bureau of Statistics (2016) reports that 25.9% of the national population were born overseas. Nearly half of those who identify as Australian (49%) were either born overseas or have one or both parents who were born overseas (Australian Bureau of Statistics, 2017). This data suggests that individuals from different cultural backgrounds will come into contact with one another, whether it be in the communities where they live, the organisations in which they work or the institutions in which they study.

As cultural diversity increases, an overwhelming majority of Australians perceive multiculturalism positively (Markus, 2017). Nonetheless, racism and racial discrimination continue to be an issue for many in the community. According to the Scanlon Foundation's Mapping Social Cohesion project (Markus, 2017), 34.2% of people surveyed from non-English speaking backgrounds had experienced discrimination in the past twelve months. Aboriginal and Torres Strait Islander people experience individual and systemic racism at higher levels still. According to the Reconciliation Barometer, 33% of Indigenous respondents reported experiencing verbal racial abuse in the previous six months (Reconciliation Australia, 2018). A commitment to combatting racism and developing cultural competence in community, workplace and university settings is imperative.

Staff at the University represent a diverse workforce comprising more than 100 different countries of home origin (personal communication, Mery Joseph, January 29, 2018). Approximately 36% of the University's student body is made up of individuals who have come to study at the University from more than 175 different countries of home origin (The University of Sydney, 2018). The University prioritises developing cultural competence in its staff and graduates, advocating that the 'organisational culture must enable each member of the University to thrive and realise their full potential' (The University of Sydney, 2016, p. 43). Cultural competence, when embedded throughout an entire system, can provide for safer, respectful and more supportive workplaces and learning environments. University staff require educational resources and tools in order to feel capable and supported in their efforts to infuse cultural competence into their context.

The NCCC's Approach to Cultural Competence Pedagogy

The NCCC aims to develop individual cultural competence capabilities whilst at the same time equipping leaders to address necessary organisational change. The NCCC's resources include a series of online modules, a massive open online course (MOOC), leadership programmes and face-to-face workshops. The in-person workshops for staff, which will be the focus of this paper, build on the information in the online modules to assist staff to develop their cultural competence capabilities. This is referred to as blended learning.

Taking a blended learning approach allows for a fusion of face-to-face and online learning experiences (Garrison & Vaughan, 2007) and provides participants with opportunities to learn both on their own and in a supportive face-to-face environment with colleagues. It also gives the NCCC facilitators the opportunity to disseminate some foundational information in the online environment, allowing for more interactive learning in the face-to-face workshops.

Blended learning also supports the NCCC's position that critical self-reflection is an important part of the journey towards cultural competence (Sherwood & Russell-Mundine, 2017). Asking participants to undertake the online modules prior to attending an in-person workshop allows time to process material and develop the skills that are necessary to critically self-reflect during and after the in-person workshops. Indeed, it is imperative for individuals to begin the cultural competence journey by reflecting on their own cultures and the ways in which these influence how they think, act and behave, before trying to understand another culture (Ranzijn McConnochie, & Nolan, 2009).

Workshop Creation

The development of the workshops was through a collaborative approach involving NCCC academics. In creating the resources, we modelled critical self-reflection, which is a fundamental capability for effective cultural competence. Built into the development process was a critical reflection cycle incorporating feedback and self-observation (Sherwood & Russell-Mundine, 2017).

Once the first iteration of each workshop was produced, pilot workshops were facilitated for colleagues within the Deputy Vice-Chancellor (Indigenous Strategy and Services) portfolio and other members and friends of the NCCC network. Participants provided formal feedback after each of the four pilot workshops in the form of survey responses in addition to feedback provided anecdotally during the sessions. The feedback was used to adjust and refine the program before making the workshops available to all University staff. When the first workshops were delivered the online modules were still in development, so each workshop was a full day in length. Following the release of the online modules and in response to feedback that full-day workshops were hard to commit to, workshops were reworked for delivery in a half-day format. Completion of the first two online modules on social and emotional wellbeing and the fundamentals of cultural competence became a pre-requisite for attending the workshops.

Workshop Structure

Developing cultural competence requires understanding a number of core components. These include understanding socialisation and worldview, one's cultural identities and critical self-reflection (National Centre for Cultural Competence, 2016). These concepts are scaffolded throughout the workshops. Each workshop has between two and four sessions that include learning outcomes, facilitator input and activities designed to support the learning outcomes and develop participants' cultural competence capabilities. There is emphasis that the journey towards cultural competence is lifelong and requires a commitment by the participants to constantly recognise and challenge their biases and assumptions.

The four foundational workshops offered by the NCCC are: (1) Cultural Competence: Social and Emotional Wellbeing; (2) Cultural Competence: The Fundamentals; (3) Cultural Competence: Relational Learning; and (4) Cultural Competence: The Foundations of Racism. The workshop on social and emotional wellbeing was designed as the starting point for University staff's journeys towards cultural competence. Drawing on an Indigenous framework, the workshop highlighted the link between having a strong sense of identity and overall wellbeing. Participants learned about identity and why it is important to understand oneself before trying to understand others and developed their resiliency skills in the context of their cultural competence journey. The second workshop introduced participants to the building blocks of cultural competence. Participants gained foundational knowledge, learned about the impact of cultural incompetence in social institutions such as higher education and developed skills to infuse cultural competence pedagogies and resources into their work.

The relational learning workshop provided teaching staff (including sessional staff) with the knowledge and resources to shift their teaching approach to facilitate student learning through a relational epistemology. Participants learned about their inter-relatedness and interdependence with each other and their broader social, political, cultural, environmental and professional contexts. Finally, the workshop on the foundations of racism introduced participants to the historical context and contemporary forms of racism in Australia and outlined the role that cultural competence can play in combating racism. Participants deepened their understanding of interpersonal and institutional racism and developed their ability to recognise, acknowledge and challenge racism when they encounter it within their work environment.

While each workshop focuses on a different topic, the overall structure of each workshop is consistent, and the content is scaffolded. Every workshop begins with an acknowledgment of country, overview of the workshop, work health and safety information, facilitator and participant introductions, and includes time for participants to write their expectations for the workshop. Participants are then introduced to the principles for engagement, in which the NCCC's overarching engagement principles are set out, discussed and agreed upon before the workshop activities commence.

Methodology

The updated in-person staff workshops were offered on a continuing basis to all University staff beginning in Semester 2, 2016. After attending an in-person workshop, participants were invited to fill out online surveys and/or participate in an in-person focus group. Participation was voluntary, and ethics approval for this research was sought and granted by the University's ethics committee. Survey data was collected from offerings of the four workshops between 2017 and 2019. A mixed-methods approach was used, asking participants to answer multiple choice, matrix/scale rating and open-ended questions. Descriptive statistics and thematic analysis were applied to analyse the data, and the information was utilised to help make improvements to the workshops. Qualitative data from a focus group held in 2016 was also included as a separate category for analysis. The voluntary nature of the workshops, and of participation in this study, resulted in a low response rate. However, data received was found to be useful in determining the effectiveness of the workshops and providing insights into particular strengths and areas for improvement going forward.

Data/Results

Online Surveys

In the social and emotional wellbeing workshop, 100% ($n = 11$) of respondents felt that initial information on the topic was provided in an effective or highly effective manner (Fig. 2.1). This suggests that participants came to the workshop with little

Fig. 2.1 Workshop effectiveness—social and emotional wellbeing

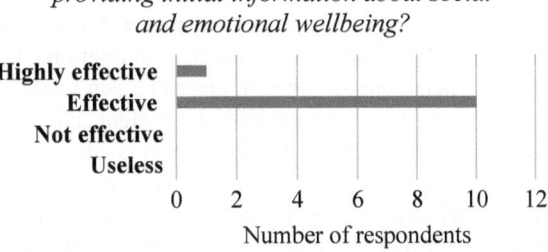

How effective was this workshop in providing initial information about social and emotional wellbeing?

Fig. 2.2 Workshop effectiveness—cultural competence capabilities

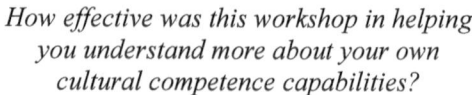

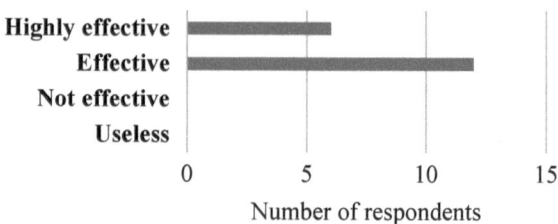

prior understanding of the concepts covered, and thus the introductory nature of the workshop was appropriate. Likewise, all respondents felt the workshop effectively helped them understand more about their own social and emotional wellbeing. After the workshop, the majority of respondents ($n = 9$) felt equipped with ideas about how to address social and emotional wellbeing in their local work context. The two neutral responses suggest that this is an area where discussion could be more effectively framed to ensure sharing of ideas among participants can help to facilitate the implementation of social and emotional wellbeing principles within the various work contexts of the University.

Similarly, those who attended the fundamentals of cultural competence workshop felt that initial information was provided effectively (highly effective: $n = 10$; effective: $n = 9$). When asked to evaluate the effectiveness of the workshop in helping them understand their personal cultural competence capabilities (Fig. 2.2), responses were positive (highly effective: $n = 6$; effective: $n = 12$). This was similarly expressed by participant's feeling equipped with information to implement cultural competence into their work (highly effective: $n = 5$; effective: $n = 13$). In the open-ended question regarding the most helpful component of the workshop, active listening and worldview activities emerged as common themes.

Analysis of feedback from the relational learning workshop provides insight into the effectiveness of the approach to teaching a pedagogical component of cultural competence. Of the 11 responses received, 100% reported that the topic was presented in a logical manner. As a topic that can be unfamiliar to staff, ensuring logical presentation and structuring of the workshop was imperative. The repeated reference to interpersonal discussions and activities as a helpful aspect of the workshop is in itself reflective of a success of the approach used, with dialogue and engaging with others being an important component of relational learning.

Feedback from the foundations of racism workshop provides important insights not only into the effectiveness of the content and facilitation but also into how racism might be experienced within and beyond the university context. All respondents ($n = 12$) found the workshop effective in providing foundational information about racism. When asked whether participants felt capable to discuss the ideas surrounding racism with their colleagues (Fig. 2.3), positive responses (strongly agree: $n = 4$;

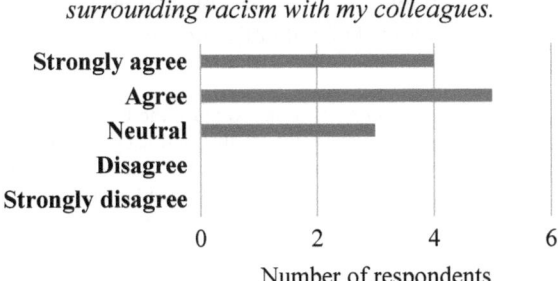

Fig. 2.3 Workshop effectiveness—racism discussion

agree: $n = 5$) were received alongside neutral responses ($n = 3$). This suggests that racism continues to permeate the higher education context and remains an area of concern for staff who seek more practical ways to engage in anti-racism work through this training.

Focus Group

A focus group was held after our first round of workshops in 2016. Three participants attended in person, while two additional participants answered the same questions via email. Two of the authors of this chapter conducted the focus group that lasted approximately 45 min. Participants were asked a number of questions related to their experience(s) of our in-person workshops, ways in which they've continued their cultural competence journeys and recommendations for improvement.

Themes

A thematic analysis of the data revealed four themes, which were (a) a desire for continued connections, (b) effectiveness, (c) a need for clarity and (d) recommendations.

a. **A desire for continued connections**

Connectedness was identified as particularly important for participants. Some participants indicated that after they finished the workshop(s), the journey seemed to halt for them. As one participant articulated:

> I really like (being) connected and would like to carry that conversation on. And you think you're going to when you walk out there, but you get back to your desk and there's emails and things to do, and then the PowerPoint gets filed there, and the workbook gets put down there.

Participants expressed that they had enjoyed the workshops and wanted to continue the collaborative journey with fellow participants after its conclusion. There was agreement that if communication between workshop participants could be continued, their cultural competence journey could progress more effectively. One participant expressed that 'it would be better for me in kind of keeping it all going if the relationships kept going.' This idea that connections to colleagues could assist in motivating participants along their cultural competence journey speaks to the need for a systems approach:

> I see the whole thing as trying to move the University's attention to these things more to centre stage, and I guess for me that will happen if people keep networking and will also happen if we can see the connection between what's happening in gender studies, what's happening in student admin, you know that kind of thing?

b. **Effectiveness**

Another theme that emerged was effectiveness. Within this theme, two of the subsections (self-reflection and peer interaction) speak to the content and structure of the in-person workshops. The third sub-section (impact on work) speaks to the follow-on effect for the participants attending one or more of the workshops.

- *Self-reflection and peer interaction*

An important component of cultural competence is critical self-reflection. To develop cultural competence, one needs to interrogate one's knowledge, how that knowledge was created and how it affects their interactions with others (Cooper, He, & Levin, 2011). Walker, Schultz and Sonn (2014, p. 200) put forward that 'cultural competence is the ability to identify and challenge one's own cultural assumptions, values and beliefs. It is about developing empathy and connected knowledge, the ability to see the world through another's eyes, or at the very least to recognise that others may view the world through a different cultural lens.' This is why self-reflection features heavily in all NCCC teaching and learning resources. A number of participants mentioned that self-reflection was a welcome part of the workshops, 'for me, [it] seemed like a good first step and it does feel like you're doing it in quite a self-reflective way.'

When asked which feature, activity or interaction in the workshop was the most helpful, a number of respondents indicated that the guided self-reflection was a powerful tool. One participant specifically noted: 'guided self-reflection and hearing stories of other members' self-reflection too clearly demonstrated the depth and complexities around what influences people's actions and perceptions.' Exposure to the worldview of others assists in moving us along our cultural competence journey. Our worldview is what guides our decision making and what helps us to make sense of the world. Behaviours and actions can stem from ones' worldview, which is why it is important to connect with others to try and learn more about where their worldview comes from (Ranzijn et al., 2009).

The workshops gave participants the opportunity to extend understanding through interactions with others: 'They [the workshops] complemented the online modules and gave me the opportunity to have very stimulating conversations and enhance my learning through those interactions.' When asked which feature, activity or interaction in the workshop was the most helpful, participants referenced interaction and exposure to others' worldviews: 'the opportunity to extend understanding through discussion and exposure to different perspectives, experiences and understandings';

'diverse conversations and different lenses that people used'; 'I so enjoyed the conversations that I've had with people here, during the workshops. And probably in ways that I never would have in a casual meeting.'

- *Impact on work*

Following participation in one or more workshop, respondents noted the impacts on the workplace: 'I've worked to embed cultural competence within the Library as a staff capability, but also as something that informs our delivery of spaces and services to be inclusive, accessible and sensitive, as articulated in our Library Strategic Plan.' Another participant remarked 'I've tried to embed material [from the workshop] in my first-year course.' Others found that participation in the workshops helped to make once abstract concepts more concrete and visible in the workplace, commenting, 'then you kind of go about your day and you see examples it or you feel examples of it that you hadn't necessarily noticed before because you didn't have the tools or the language around it.'

c. **A need for clarity**

Another theme that came through was participants' desire for clarity. As the NCCC worked to create and disseminate the workshops as a component of the suite of resources, the way those resources 'fit together' seemed confusing for those outside of the NCCC. One participant commented, 'I just felt like the way it was presented I couldn't actually work out how the four courses fitted [sic] together.' There also seemed to be confusion around who the workshops were meant for. Professional and academic staff were encouraged to attend, but this was unclear to participants, with it being remarked, 'I was a bit like 'Is that actually something I can go to?' This was expressed by another participant:

> I looked at the other ones and they looked a little bit abstract or a little bit ambiguous – I'm glad you used that word. Because I was a bit like 'Oh why do they apply to me? I don't really get that.' So, I didn't really know how they fit it into the online modules as well.

d. **Recommendations**

Our focus group and survey respondents shared a number of recommendations with us, many of which have since been implemented. One of the most salient recommendations was participants' interest in having a clear connection between our workshops (how they fit together, why the specific topics), and how the workshops then fit in with the suite of resources overall.

Respondents also recommended that the online modules and in-person workshops be combined in some way. From this recommendation, some content was removed from the *Cultural Competence: The Fundamentals* workshop that was covered in the first two online modules, and then made completion of the first two online modules a pre-requisite for attendance at any of the face-to-face workshops. This has helped to allay another issue, which was that participants would come to the sessions with varying levels of understanding about cultural competence. Requiring participants to complete the online modules before attending in person ensured that participants were on the same base-line level from which to continue their journey.

Another important recommendation was to further utilise the strategic plan and graduate attributes. The University's *2016–20 Strategic Plan* calls on the campus community to embed cultural competence into the culture of the University, as well as into the student curriculum. This recommendation reminded us that not everyone on campus may be aware of the strategic plan or what is included in it. Its promotion as a tool for participants to utilise as they continue their cultural competence journey is thus imperative, as the systems-level support is what will enable the embedding of cultural competence into all aspects of the University.

Limitations

The small sample size is a limitation of this study. This limitation can be explained by the voluntary nature of participation in the workshops and research study. Going forward, longitudinal research should be undertaken to assess workshop effectiveness over time and within various contexts across campus (academic and staff spaces).

Conclusion

This study sought to determine the effectiveness of workshops in the development of staff cultural competence at an Australian higher education institution. Analysis of the survey and focus group data found that the workshops were effective in educating participants about various aspects of cultural competence, including social and emotional wellbeing, the fundamentals of cultural competence, relational learning and the foundations of racism. Our workshops do not seek to provide a 'tick-a-box' solution. The findings of this research leave us optimistic that the NCCC resources are forming an integral part of driving cultural change within this tertiary setting.

References

Australian Bureau of Statistics. (2016). *Data by region.* Retrieved from http://stat.abs.gov.au/itt/r.jsp?databyregion&ref=CTA2#/.

Australian Bureau of Statistics. (2017). 'Census reveals a fast changing, culturally diverse nation' (Media Release, 27 June 2017). Retrieved from http://www.abs.gov.au/ausstats/abs@.nsf/lookup/Media%20Release3.

Australian Government—Department of Home Affairs. (2017). *Multicultural Australia: United, Strong, Successful.* Retrieved from https://www.homeaffairs.gov.au/LifeinAustralia/Documents/MulticulturalAffairs/english-multicultural-statement.pdf.

Cooper, J. E., He, Y., & Levin, B. B. (2011). *Who I am: How can we understand ourselves as cultural beings? In Developing Critical Cultural Competence: A Guide for 21 Century Educators.* Thousand Oaks, California: Corwin Press.

Cross, T., Bazron, B. J., Dennis, K. W., & Isaacs, M. R. (1989). *Towards a Culturally Competent System of Care: A monograph on effective services for minority children who are severely emotionally disturbed.* Washington DC: CASSP Technical Assistance Center, Georgetown University Child Development Center.

Garrison, D. R., & Vaughan, N. D. (2007). *Blended learning in higher education.* San Francisco: Jossey-Bass.

Kirmayer, L. J. (2012). Rethinking cultural competence. *Transcultural Psychiatry, 49*(2), 149–164.

Markus, A. (2017). *Mapping Social Cohesion: The Scanlon Foundation surveys 2017.* Retrieved from http://scanlonfoundation.org.au/socialcohesion2017/.

National Centre for Cultural Competence. (2016). *What is cultural competence?* Retrieved from https://sydney.edu.au/nccc/about-us/what-is-cultural-competence.html.

Ranzijn, R., McConnochie, K., & Nolan, W. (2009). *Psychology and Indigenous Australians: foundations of cultural competence.* Victoria: Palgrave Macmillan.

Reconciliation Australia. (2018). *Australian Reconciliation Barometer 2018.* Retrieved from https://www.reconciliation.org.au/wp-content/uploads/2019/02/ra_2019-barometer-brochure_web.single.page_.pdf.

Sherwood, J., & Russell-Mundine, G. (2017). How we do business: Setting the agenda for cultural competence at the University of Sydney. In J. Frawley, S. Larkin, & J. A. Smith (Eds.), *Indigenous pathways, transitions and participation in higher education: From policy to practice* (pp. 133–150). Singapore: Springer Open.

The University of Sydney. (2018). *Enrolment countries.* Sydney, NSW: The University of Sydney.

The University of Sydney. (2016). 2016–20 Strategic Plan. Retrieved from https://sydney.edu.au/about-us/vision-and-values/strategy.html.

The University of Sydney. (2012). Wingara Mura—Bunga Barrabuggu: The University of Sydney Aboriginal and Torres Strait Islander Integrated Strategy. Retrieved from http://sydney.edu.au/strategy/docs/wingara-mura-bunga-barrabugu.pdf.

Universities Australia. (2011). National Best Practice Framework for Indigenous Cultural Competency in Australian Universities. Retrieved from http://www.indigenousculturalcompetency.edu.au/index.html.

Walker, R., Schultz, C., & Sonn, C. (2014). Cultural Competence—Transforming Policy, Services, Programs and Practice. In P. Dudgeon, H. Milroy, & R. Walker (Eds.), *Working together: Aboriginal and Torres Strait Islander mental health and wellbeing principles and practice.* Australian Institute of Health and Welfare: Canberra, ACT.

Chapter 3
Methodology for Evaluating the University of Sydney's Culturally Competent Leadership Program

Alessandra Pecci, Jack Frawley, and Tran Nguyen

Abstract This chapter discusses the methodology employed to evaluate the University of Sydney's Culturally Competent Leadership Program (CCLP). The CCLP is an internal staff professional development project hosted and delivered by the National Centre for Cultural Competence (NCCC). The CCLP aims to develop and support cultural competence champions and practices across the University, and to create a university-wide network of empowered and engaged leaders committed to nurturing the development of successive generations of champions. In line with the University of Sydney's strategic commitment to developing leaders at all levels, this program forms part of the collective commitment to embedding cultural competence into all facets of the University's work. Built into the inaugural CCLP was an evaluation system that evaluated the program's relevance, effectiveness, efficiency, impact and sustainability. Since 2017, the CCLP program has been delivered to the University staff by the NCCC for three consecutive years. Data used in this chapter was collected in the inaugural program.

Keywords Cultural competence · Culturally competent leadership · Professional development · Program evaluation

Introduction

The evaluation of the Culturally Competent Leadership Program (CCLP) had three distinct aims:

1. To appraise the achievements of CCLP objectives;
2. To assess the soundness of the CCLP approach and component strategies, and analyse their respective performance in relation to achieving targeted objectives and sustainability of results achieved; and,

A. Pecci (✉)
Faculty of Society and Design, Bond University, Gold Coast, QLD, Australia
e-mail: apecci@bond.edu.au

J. Frawley · T. Nguyen
National Centre for Cultural Competence, The University of Sydney, Sydney, NSW, Australia

© The Author(s) 2020

J. Frawley et al. (eds.), *Transforming Lives and Systems*,
SpringerBriefs in Education, https://doi.org/10.1007/978-981-15-5351-6_3

3. To analyse constraints, lessons learned, the use of evidence-based best practices and evaluate the strategic opportunity to build upon achievements to inform further CCLPs.

The discussion in this chapter begins with a background context to the CCLP, including a synthesis of the reviewed literature on culturally competent leadership, and the rationale for cultural competence in the Australian higher education sector. The chapter then outlines the program's goals, objectives and intended outputs, as well as an overview of its structure and format. The remainder of the chapter focuses on the evaluation of the CCLP, which covers the methodology employed and the evaluation implementation undertaken.

Program Context and Background

The University of Sydney's Strategic Plan 2020 emphasises the development of cultural competence for all staff and builds leadership quality in this area. It states that the university is 'committed to a series of actions to… develop (staff) capacity as agents of cultural change' (p. 44), and that 'staff have a particular responsibility to… demonstrate leadership in this area' (p. 43). The Strategic Plan (p. 13) states specifically that academic staff should:

> participate effectively in intercultural settings in research, in the classroom, and in the day-to-day life of the University. They should be open to a diversity of ways of being, doing and knowing, as well as looking for, and understanding, the context of those engaged in, or affected by, our research and education.

The Strategic Plan also embeds cultural competence as a graduate quality in all undergraduate degrees and commits to collaborating with the NCCC on skills development 'through a shared commitment to a more collective, relational model for learning and teaching, [and to] embed the development of cultural competence in the curriculum' (p. 36).

The University of Sydney has also acknowledged 'the inherent rights of Aboriginal and Torres Strait Islander peoples to be self-determined and respected as Australia's first peoples' (Sherwood & Russell-Mundine, 2017, p. 134) through the *Wingara Mura–Bunga Barrabugu* ('Wingara Mura'), the University's Aboriginal and Torres Strait Islander Integrated Strategy. Wingara Mura establishes as a key student and staff capability and the ability to engage effectively, respectfully and productively in critical thinking and self-reflection regarding Aboriginal and Torres Strait Islander issues specifically, and diversity more broadly. As Sherwood and Russell-Mundine (2017, p. 134) note:

> Wingara Mura places the promotion of Aboriginal and Torres Strait Islander participation, engagement, education and research as a core objective of the University. Within this policy context, the NCCC aims to provide the essential framework to embed the cultural competence qualities necessary to implement the strategy across the organisation, its staff and students.

The NCCC follows and aligns its cultural competence agenda with the recommendations of Universities Australia (2011). These recommendations position universities as agents of change, not only in improving higher education outcomes, including access and participation, for Indigenous Australians within the universities, but also by making 'a commitment to the capacity building of Indigenous communities' (p. 17). The NCCC locates its understanding of cultural competence very much in the context of addressing social justice issues, such as equity, access and participation in higher education, as the foundations to creating change.

Cultural competence can lay the foundations for a socially-just consciousness and culturally diverse, respectful worldviews, grown through the development and processing of core values, knowledge, behaviours and actions. Its principles and praxis have germinated through the work of Indigenous and culturally diverse scholars, health professionals, peoples and groups whose work has been based upon a human rights agenda focused on equity and justice (Cross, Bazron, Dennis, & Isaacs, 1989; Ranzin, McConnochie & Nolan, 2009; Sherwood et al., 2011; Universities Australia, 2011). The embedding of cultural competence requires deep, transformational change in behaviour, teaching and learning, a deeper institution-wide commitment to the values espoused by the University, and an investment in developing a more understanding and respectful university culture and organisational relationships. It also requires a depth of knowledge and strong, informed leadership in the field of cultural competence to support the transformational change the University wants to achieve.

The literature presents culturally competent leadership as an underlying set of attributes, skills and behaviours, as well as knowledge, that run across, and are foundational to the wide range of designations featuring in the scholarship. Culturally competent leadership is transformative/transformational, values-driven, moral, critically self-reflective (Terrell & Lindsey, 2008; Beachum, 2011) and purposeful, in its intent and scope. Leadership in this space equates to courage, advocacy for social justice and human rights, and a willingness and ability for reflexive practice and self-awareness. Culturally competent leaders in higher education settings display characteristics of 'civility, ethical behaviour, data-driven decision-making and cultural sensitivity' (Thompson et al., 2017, p. 79). It is the type of leadership that is required if the academy is to create more inclusive, culturally competent university communities. Leadership in this sense is seen to drive and enable transformation and change, and the notion of agency, at the institutional, organisational, as well as at the individual level, underpins culturally competent leadership. Leaders in this space work to identify, transform and question systems that generate inequity, disparity and social injustice (Horsford et al., 2011; Su & Wood, 2017; Shultz & Viczko, 2016). The moral imperative that accompanies culturally competent leadership also underpins theories of transformative leadership (Shields, 2010; Marbley et al., 2015) and foregrounds the concepts of agency (Komives & Wagner, 2016) and transformative action in leadership discourse and practice. Educational leaders in this space need to commit to critical conversations around the historical, social and material legacies of colonial practices, if they wish to enact systemic change and transformation. Shultz and Viczko (2016, p. 2) note, for example, that even higher education institutions 'have not escaped this [colonial] legacy, and the durability of issues and intersections of race, gender, and class violence are evident in our organisations'. On the criticality of the systems that perpetuate longstanding injustices, López (2016, p. 20) asserts that 'educational leaders who ground their work in critical perspectives seek to create social change by challenging the status quo and systems of power that dominate and subjugate'. Transformative, culturally competent leadership hence focuses on systemic change and critically illuminating, through the unpacking of systems, inadvertently held power and privilege, disparity, inequity and injustice.

In Australia, cultural competence in higher education cannot be separated from social justice, human rights, equity, equal opportunity and reconciliation discourse as it relates to Australia's First Nations Peoples, and hence Aboriginal and Torres Strait Islander students and staff. To this end, within the Australian higher education sector, cultural competence has been defined as:

> Student and staff knowledge and understanding of Indigenous Australian cultures, histories and contemporary realities and awareness of Indigenous protocols, combined with the proficiency to engage and work effectively in Indigenous contexts congruent to the expectations of Indigenous Australian peoples … [and] the ability to critically reflect on one's own culture and professional paradigms in order to understand its cultural limitations and effect positive change. (Universities Australia, 2011, p. 3)

Developing cultural capabilities within the higher education sector hence requires leaders, in traditional leadership roles as well as individual advocates and champions who may not necessarily hold senior leadership titles, to guide a whole-of-institution approach involving the systemic, organisational, professional and individual realms (Miralles & Migliorino, 2005). This 'includes examining individual attitudes and practice in teaching as well as management, executive, policy and strategic commitment to revise and assess capacity to implement culturally competent teaching, learning, academic, research and employment spaces' (Taylor, Durey, Mulcock, Kickett, & Jones, 2014, p. 37).

Universities Australia's 2011 *National Best Practice Framework for Indigenous Cultural Competency in Australian Universities* has been instrumental in providing guidance and direction on good and best practice strategies, approaches and methodologies to embed cultural competence across higher education institutions. Progress with embracing cultural competence in higher education in Australia has been incremental and uneven. The findings of the *Review of Higher Education Access and Outcomes for Aboriginal and Torres Strait Islander People* (Bradley, Noonan, Nugent, & Scales, 2008) reveal that there remains significant work to be done on embedding cultural competence at a whole-of-institution level. Leadership in all of the domains (institutional, organisational, professional and individual) is seen as fundamental to bringing about the cultural change which is being called for.

Overview of the Culturally Competent Leadership Program

The CCLP was launched in February 2017, a first-of-a-kind professional development leadership program open to both professional and academic staff across the University of Sydney. Led by the NCCC, in itself a community of leaders of cultural competence dedicated to enacting the transformational change the University wants to achieve, the program materialised the University's strategic vision and dedication to leadership initiatives in the cultural competence space by establishing and supporting a network or community of practice of cultural competence champions, who commit to leading initiatives in their local contexts. This type of individual agency was seen to complement leadership initiatives at the organisational and systemic level, and represented a bottom-up approach of sorts, seen as vital to achieving the University's stated vision of cultural change and transformation. The common attributes, behaviours, knowledge and skills of culturally competent leaders identified in previous sections of the literature review informed, in many ways, the vision of the CCLP.

The transformation and change envisaged by the University of Sydney requires leadership that is open and committed to resilient sense of self through a reflective cycle of thinking and developing a critical reflective praxis, intra-personally or with the self, and inter-personally or with others. Praxis:

> involves the continual, dynamic interaction among knowledge acquisition, deep reflection, and action at two levels - the intrapersonal and the extra-personal - with the purpose of transformation and paradigmatic change. At the intrapersonal level, praxis involves self-knowledge, critical self-reflection, and acting to transform oneself as a leader for social justice. At the extra-personal level, praxis involves knowing and understanding systemic social justice issues, reflecting on these issues, and taking action to address them (Furman, 2012, p. 203).

Culturally competent leadership requires critical approaches to the systems and paradigms that continue to perpetuate injustices, as much as it requires critical self-reflection and a personal journey of learning and transformation.

Culturally Competent Leadership Program Aims and Themes

The aims of the CCLP were to:

1. Develop influential leaders who will build resilience for change through the support of the broader network of leaders;
2. Develop influential leaders who will engage with a new and innovative discourse of culturally competent leadership;
3. Create a university-wide network or a community-of-practice of empowered and engaged leaders committed to nurturing the development of successive generations of culturally competent leaders.

The CCLP consisted of four themes to address the aims of the program:

1. **Cultural competence**: the ability to participate ethically and effectively in personal and professional intercultural settings.

Cultural competence, from an Australian perspective, acknowledges that it is built on Indigenous foundation that is informed through Indigenous ways of knowing, being and doing. Universities Australia (2011, p. 171) asserts that Indigenous cultural competence requires an organisational culture which is committed to social justice, human rights and the process of reconciliation through valuing and supporting Indigenous cultures, knowledges and peoples as integral to the core business of the institution.

2. **Leadership praxis**: leadership is viewed and experienced as both reflection and practice.

To lead within a culturally competent framework requires leaders who develop a more explicit moral literacy with respect to situations in which their organisations engage in cultural change. This requires leaders who are capable of exploring their own sense of moral purpose in their work through critical reflection; appreciate the importance of culture in leading ethically; and, understand the power of moral purpose as a mobiliser of practice. This type of leadership is integral to building culturally competent leaders.

3. **Communities of practice (or networks)**: a community of leaders who care about cultural competence and share in its practice.

A community of practice in the context of CCLP is one in which there is support for cultural competence; that creates a common ground and sense of common identity built on a cultural competence foundation; where there is a community of committed leaders who care about cultural competence and create the social fabric of learning around it; and, where there is shared effective practice. This requires a united structure and approach, and connection with others.

4. **Critical reflection**: challenges the learner to question assumptions, beliefs and commonly accepted knowledge and to actively participate in what they learn.

Critical reflection involves a critique of the presuppositions on which beliefs have been built. The capacity to reflect relates to how effectively individuals can learn from their personal experiences. Critical reflection therefore provides a meaningful way for leaders to gain genuine understanding. Culturally competent leaders should be highly skilled in critical reflection theory and practice.

Culturally Competent Leadership Program Phases

Phase 1: Self-nomination and selection of participants
NCCC academic staff set out in the first phase of the program to engage and consult with faculty Deans and divisional/departmental Directors. These preliminary conversations aimed to introduce senior leaders and decision-makers to the program,

respond to any queries, concerns and suggestions, and encourage them to promote the program widely across their faculties and divisions/departments. Interested staff, both professional and academic, self-nominated and applied by submitting an expression of interest to their Dean or Director, who then in turn selected a maximum of five applicants based on internal selection criteria and forwarded the list to the CCLP team. Deans and Directors were required to commit to supporting nominees to be available for the entire program. The NCCC was not involved in the selection process, aside from suggesting possible criteria for consideration, including the following:

1. Be passionate about promoting cultural competence and actively coaching and mentoring others;
2. Willingness and ability to consult and collaborate with others, balancing this with a preference for making decisions;
3. Be comfortable dealing with other staff, forming new relationships, and at ease expressing opinions; and,
4. Be working towards completing the NCCC online cultural competence modules before the retreat.

Phase 2: Program launch

The NCCC hosted a program launch event, which involved an introductory workshop on cultural competence in the higher education context and the call for leadership at all levels of the university community to participate. This was followed by a networking event with participants, NCCC staff, and other relevant stakeholders from the University of Sydney that informed the CCLP education program.

Phase 3: Off-site residential program

Sixty-six CCLP participants, including both academic and professional staff from across the University's faculties and departments, attended a three-day off-site residential program in South Durras, New South Wales (Fig. 3.1). Sessions focused on building participants' capabilities in critical self-reflection, on building knowledge in cultural competence discourse through theory and practice, including leadership discourse, and on exploring concepts of communities of practice. Participants were also led through a future casting session, planning for how they might embed what they learned through the residential program into their local contexts, and into the business of the University. Participants also had the opportunity to spend a half day with members of the local Indigenous community.

Phase 4: NCCC workshops

After the CCLP retreats, participants were invited to participate in a series of NCCC workshops that would build their cultural competence knowledge-base, as well as their confidence in practicing and championing cultural competence in their local contexts.

Phase 5: Ongoing engagement and support

Following the off-site residential program, and in conjunction with the roll-out of NCCC workshops, the CCLP team, at the suggestion of participants, organised monthly networking sessions as an opportunity for participants to reconvene and share information and ideas on embedding cultural competence in their local contexts.

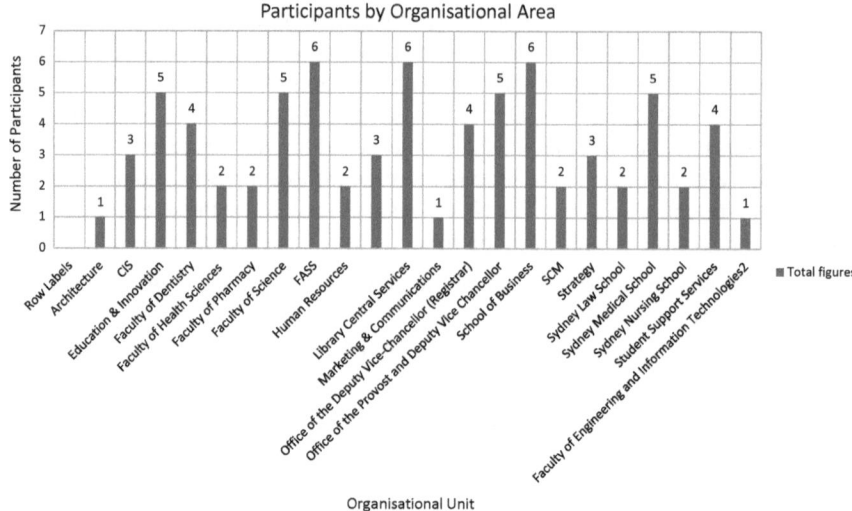

Fig. 3.1 Participation of staff by organisational units

Evaluation Methodology

A responsive evaluation approach (Stake, 1967; Stake & Abma, 2005; Abma, 2005) incorporating process and outcome dimensions was adopted for the evaluation. Stake (1967) argues that evaluated programs can include different stakeholders who share different views, perspectives and expectations. Therefore, it is the responsibility of evaluators to acknowledge such diversity when designing the evaluation of programs or activities. According to Abma (2005, p. 288), 'responsive evaluation does not only deliver evidence in time, but also evidence that is context-bound. It produces local knowledge that enables practitioners to use it in their context, in a specific case'.

The evaluation of CCLP was considered a collaborative partnership in that it equitably involved participants and evaluators in the evaluation process. Participants contributed their experience of the CCLP, and the knowledge gained will be incorporated into action for the next reiteration of the CCLP. The evaluation recognised the participants as a social and cultural entity, in the sense that they are all members of the University community and are actively engaged in the evaluation process. In line with the responsive evaluation approach, processes and outcomes were identified, documented, analysed and evaluated, considering the experiences and perspectives of the participants. The evaluation was guided by the following principles:

- Recognise the participants as a unit of identity;
- Build on strengths and resources within the University community;
- Facilitate collaborative, equitable involvement of all partners in the evaluation; and,
- Integrate knowledge and action for mutual benefit of the University community.

Research and Evaluation Plan and Procedures

The following steps were undertaken in developing the research plan:

1. Establish the evaluation team;
2. Formulate the research aims; and
3. Identify the research design and program logic framework.

Ethics Procedure

The CCLP research team gained research ethics approval from the University's Human Research Ethics Committee (HREC) at the onset of the program. Some minor clarifications and additional information were sought by the HREC in the first instance, and these were reviewed and approved shortly after submission, and research activities commenced thereafter. Participation in the research and evaluation of the CCLP was on a voluntary basis, and program participants were made aware of the research and evaluation project prior to the off-site residential phase. All program participants received a Participant Information Statement (outlining the breadth, scope, methodology of the evaluation) as well as a Participant Consent Form, through which they were to provide written consent to participating in the research and evaluation activities throughout the life-time of the program.

Evaluation Logical Framework

A logical framework, or log-frame was developed for the CCLP evaluation, detailing the evaluation's goals, activities and anticipated results *vis-á-vis* the CCLP's over-arching aims. The log-frame was viewed as a tool for improving the planning, implementation, management, monitoring and evaluation of the CCLP (see Appendix 1).

Evaluation Aims

As mentioned in the beginning of this chapter, the evaluation of the CCLP had three distinct aims:

1. To appraise the achievements of CCLP objectives;
2. To assess the soundness of the CCLP approach and component strategies, and analyse their respective performance in relation to achieving targeted objectives and sustainability of results achieved; and,

3. To analyse constraints, lessons learned, the use of evidence-based best practices and evaluate the strategic opportunity to build upon achievements to inform further CCLPs.

Evaluation Design and Data Collection

The evaluation utilised a mixed-methods design that included pre- and post-program surveys; participant focus groups; and, participant interviews (one-on-one). A total of sixty-six staff, professional and academic combined, participated in the CCLP. The two surveys were conducted online, through the *Survey Monkey* platform—one prior to the residential, and one at its conclusion. Key informant interviews and focus group discussions were held at the end of the program, and were audio-recorded, and subsequently transcribed. Personal names and other forms of identification were redacted to ensure anonymity, and any publications disseminating the results were de-identified.

Data Analysis

The evaluation data was analysed utilising the following five criteria:

1. Relevance: the extent to which the CCLP objectives are consistent with the University's needs, priorities and policies.
2. Effectiveness: the extent to which the CCLP aims were achieved or are expected to be achieved.
3. Efficiency: the extent to which the CCLP activities were achieved within the allocated budget.
4. Sustainability: the extent to which the benefits from the CCLP continue after its completion.
5. Impact: the effects produced by the CCLP.

Online survey data, for both the pre- and post-residential phase of the program, was analysed in the first instance by two members of the research team. Raw data was initially exported from the *Survey Monkey* online platform and interpreted/analysed by the Chief Investigator who relayed findings in a summary document. This document was circulated amongst the research team, along with the exported raw data, for review and comment to ensure consensus in its interpretation. Focus group discussions and individual informant interviews were audio-recorded, and subsequently transcribed by professional transcription services, outsourced. Members of the research team reviewed and analysed the transcripts individually and subsequently convened to share their individual findings and reach a general consensus on these findings. Content analysis was undertaken by coding the content under the predetermined themes of relevance, effectiveness, efficiency, sustainability and impact.

The process was undertaken by two individual researchers and these findings were reviewed by a third researcher.

Discussion and Conclusion

The inaugural CCLP had a very bold and ambitious vision in creating its first generation of leaders, who would be committed to championing the cultural competence agenda and leading initiatives within their local settings—there are as many successes to be celebrated as there are lessons to be learned, as the evaluation of the CCLP has revealed. At a glance, program evaluation participants highlighted a series of program successes, particularly as they relate to the residential component, in that it:

- engendered transformation at the individual, personal level through experiential learning opportunities and critical self-reflection activities that facilitates better understanding about Indigenous history, cultures and social issues, appropriate engagement with Indigenous peoples, as well as the importance of cultural competence;
- facilitated relationship-building and nurturing amongst and between participants;
- developed foundational knowledge of cultural competence for participants, and hence equipping them with the confidence they needed to champion the agenda;
- created a desire for ongoing learning and gaining further knowledge; and
- developed a relationship with the NCCC and its staff resulting in an enhancement of the CCLP networks.

As stated in the introduction of this chapter, the evaluation sets out to appraise the achievements of the CCLP key objectives that include the development of culturally competent leaders and the creation of a university-wide network or a community of practice of such leaders. The appraisal of these objectives has revealed that the program succeeded in creating and developing a network of cultural competence champions. The inaugural CCLP certainly engendered transformation and shifts at the individual level, facilitated relationship-building amongst and between participants, and developed the majority of participants' foundational knowledge in culturally competence discourse and in culturally competent leadership discourse, creating a desire for ongoing learning and gaining more knowledge. The majority of respondents in the post-retreat survey (21/29 participants) felt 'relatively' confident that they will have an impact on embedding cultural competence on the local context post-treat. Seven of the remaining respondents felt 'very' confident.

The evaluation's appraisal of NCCC staff facilitation of the CCLP has shown that the methods, approaches, processes and content have met program participants' expectations, hence setting the benchmark for future CCLPs. What the evaluation also revealed was the CCLP facilitator team's ability to respond to participant suggestions and feedback through progressive program revision and streamlining. Feedback to date has demonstrated that participants are now networked, engaged, and conversing on an ongoing basis, through diverse channels, sharing their local stories and practice with the broader community of champions.

Limitations

It is also important to note that the evaluation itself had limitations in terms of:

1. Measuring impact: in the absence of standard cultural competence measures of success in higher education contexts, it is difficult to determine the extent to which professional development programs like the CCLP have impacts on the University's path to becoming culturally competent.
2. Data collection methods: it is worth highlighting that while the data collection instruments gathered sufficient data for this evaluation, further methods would have added useful data through participant observation and non-participant observation. In participant observation one member of the evaluation team could have taken an active role in the program, from the beginning phase to the end, which would provide an insider viewpoint and generate rich data. Additionally, one member of the evaluation team could take on the role of a non-participant observer, observing the CCLP activities but without taking an active part.
3. Potential bias of the research team: the Chief Investigator for the evaluation, who conducted interviews and focus group data collections and analysed the data, was also a staff member contributing to the CCLP retreats. This presented a level of potential bias. To mitigate this, two more levels of data analysis were undertaken by two NCCC academic staff who were independent of all of the CCLP design and delivery.

Conclusion

The responsive evaluation approach (Stake, 1967; Abma, 2005) requires evaluators to consider different perspectives and values of the program's stakeholders. In the evaluation of the CCLP program, different measures were adopted in order to enable the evaluators to capture the diversity in terms of the participants' perspectives and values towards cultural competence in general and the CCLP program in particular. The evaluation acknowledged the diversity of participants who shared different views, perspectives and expectations, as well as holding a variety of positions including academic and professional staff. Participants were invited to join the pre- and post-program surveys, focus groups as well as one-on-one interviews. As a result, data collected from those evaluation methods allowed the evaluators to better understand the participants' different as well as similar perspectives and values. The use of the pre- and post-program surveys was both valuable and effective as it helped to reveal, in part, any cognitive or emotional changes that participants may have after joining the CCLP program.

Many participants acknowledged significant transformation at the individual level in terms of engaging with Indigenous peoples and views towards cultural competence. Those findings allowed the evaluators to acknowledge one significant contribution of the CCLP program as well as the achievement of the program's objectives: to develop influential leaders who will engage with a new and innovative discourse of culturally competent leadership. CCLP participants' transformation, as revealed via the post-program survey, focus groups and one-one-one interview, is a good starting point to developing culturally competent leaders. It is because such transformation can allow leaders to identify and question systems that generate inequity, disparity and social injustice (Horsford et al., 2011; Su & Wood, 2017).

The design used for the CCLP evaluation has shown that the questions, data sources and data collection methods were adequate to address the evaluation aims. The design involved the participants as partners in the evaluation, building on their strengths and resources and integrating their knowledge and perspectives for mutual benefit of the University community. This evaluation approach considers the full context of participants, rather than seeing them in isolation from the University environment, culture, and identity

The key advantages of the evaluation design included enhancing the relevance and use of the evaluation data by the CCLP team and improving the quality and validity of evaluation by incorporating the knowledge and experiences of the participants. The findings of this evaluation should assist the University to continue to address the professional development needs of its staff in the area of cultural competence.

Appendix 1

Evaluation Aims

1. To appraise the achievements of CCLP objectives.
2. To assess the soundness of the CCLP approach and component strategies, and analyse their respective performance in relation to achieving targeted objectives and sustainability of results achieved.
3. To analyse constraints, lessons learned, the use of evidence-based best practices and evaluate the strategic opportunity to build upon achievements to inform further CCLPs.

Stakeholders and Beneficiaries:
Participants, NCCC, University of Sydney

Evaluation criteria	Data sources	Data collection	Data analysis & reporting	Short term outcomes
Relevance Effectiveness Impact Sustainability Efficiency	Participants	Surveys Focus group discussions	Qualitative data content analysis Quantitative data descriptive analysis Reporting: findings & recommendations	Engaged, capable and culturally competent leaders Revised CCLPs Extended network

Key Questions

1. How effective was the CCLP in addressing the participants' understanding of the relevance of cultural competence for the University of Sydney's strategic policies and plans?
2. How effective was the CCLP in changing the participants' understanding of cultural competence capabilities in the university context?
3. As a result of participating in the CCLP did participants develop leadership capabilities with respect to cultural competence and a greater understanding of Indigeneity, diversity and difference?
4. Did the program equip participants with the knowledge and practical skills to develop cultural competence innovations and activities in your own work contexts?

Survey pre-workshops	Survey post-residential	Focus groups
Relevance		
To what extent do you believe that the program will assist in developing your understanding of cultural competence?	To what extent did the program meet your expectations?	Describe how the activities and outputs of the CCLP to date have achieved their intended aims, which are to provide participants with:
How relevant is the program for your professional development?	What specific activities were useful in assisting your development of cultural competency?	A deeper understanding of culturally competent leadership in the University context;
What is your level of understanding of cultural competence to University policy?	To what extent did the program assist in developing your understanding of cultural competency to University policy?	Development of respectful leadership capabilities sensitive to Indigeneity, diversity and difference; Increased capability to lead cultural competence
What is your level of understanding of communities of practice and how these professional communities can be used across the university?	To what extent did the program assist in developing your understanding of communities of practice?	innovations in their own work contexts; and Support and peer mentoring from the CCLP cohort

(continued)

(continued)

Survey pre-workshops	Survey post-residential	Focus groups
Effectiveness		
To what extent should your skills and knowledge be used in the design and delivery of program?	How effective were your skills and knowledge used in the program?	How did the retreat and the post-retreat workshop enable your planning for a future roll-out of cultural competence praxis in your local context? Which aspects worked, and which aspects need improvement?
How would you rate yourself as a culturally competent leader?	Overall how effective was the program in preparing you as a cultural competent leader?	
Impact		
To what extent will the program impact on you as a culturally competent leader?	Overall, what was the impact of the program on you as a culturally competent leader?	How would you describe the impact the CCLP has had thus far on you, individually and professionally? What impact do you see the CCLP having on organisational culture in the medium and long-term? What is needed to ensure the CCLP will have this impact?
How much of an impact do you feel your involvement in the program will have on embedding cultural competence across the University?	How confident are you that you will have an impact on embedding cultural competence across the University?	
Sustainability		
What do you believe are the major factors that will make cultural competence sustainable across the University?	Overall, how confident are you that you can contribute to the sustainability of cultural competence across the University?	What is required to ensure the CCLP's durability and sustainability? What are the enabling farces (existing and/or prospective) that will ensure the program's sustainability? What are the disabling forces (existing and/or prospective) that threaten the program's sustainability?

References

Abma, T. (2005). Responsive evaluation: Its meaning and special contribution to health promotion. *Evaluation and Program Planning, 28*, 279–289.

Beachum, F. (2011). Culturally relevant leadership for complex 21st century school contexts. *The SAGE handbook of educational leadership: Advances in theory, research, and practice*, 26–35.

Bradley, D., Noonan, P., Nugent, H., & Scales, B. (2008). *Review of Australian higher education: Final report*. Canberra, A.C.T: Department of Education, Employment and Workplace Relations.

Cross, T., Bazron, B. J., Dennis, K. W., & Isaacs, M. R. (1989). *Towards a Culturally Competent System of Care: A monograph on effective services for minority children who are severely emotionally disturbed*. Washington DC: CASSP Technical Assistance Center, Georgetown University Child Development Center.

Furman, G. (2012). Social justice leadership as praxis: Developing capacities through preparation programs. *Educational Administration Quarterly, 48*(2), 191–229.

Horsford, S. D., Grosland, T., & Gunn, K. M. (2011). Pedagogy of the personal and professional: Toward a framework for culturally relevant leadership. *Journal of School Leadership, 21*(4), 582–606.

Komives, S. R., & Wagner, W. (Eds.). (2016). *Leadership for a better world: Understanding the social change model of leadership development*. John Wiley & Sons.

López, A. E. (2016). *Culturally responsive and socially just leadership in diverse contexts: From theory to action*. Singapore: Springer.

Marbley, A. F., Bonner, F. A., II, Robinson, P. A., Stevens, H., Li, J., Phelan, K., et al. (2015). Voices from the field of social justice: defining moments in our professional journeys. *Multicultural Education, 23*(1), 45.

Miralles, J., & Migliorino, P. (2005). *Discussion paper: Increasing cultural competency for healthier living*. Canberra: National Health and Medical Research Council.

Ranzijn, R., McConnochie, K., & Nolan, W. (Eds.). (2009). *Psychology and Indigenous Australians: Effective teaching and practice*. Cambridge Scholars Publishing.

Sherwood, J., Keech, S., Keenan, T., & Kelly, B. (2011). Indigenous studies: Teaching and learning together. In N. Purdie, G. Milgate, & H. Rachel Bell (Eds.), *Two-way teaching and learning: Toward culturally reflective and relevant education* (pp. 189–204). Melbourne: ACER Press.

Sherwood, J., & Russell-Mundine, G. (2017). How we do business: Setting the agenda for cultural competence at The University of Sydney. In J. Frawley, S. Larkin & J. A. Smith (Eds.), *Indigenous pathways, transitions and participation in higher education: From policy to practice*. Singapore: Springer Open.

Shields, C. M. (2010). Transformative leadership: Working for equity in diverse contexts. *Educational Administration Quarterly, 46*(4), 558–589.

Shultz, L., & Viczko, M. (2016). Global social justice, democracy and leadership of higher education: An introduction. In *Assembling and Governing the Higher Education Institution*. London: Palgrave Macmillan.

Stake, B. (1967). The countenance of educational evaluation. *Teachers College Record, 68*(7), 523–540.

Stake, R. E., & Abma, T. A. (2005). Responsive evaluation. In S. Mathison (Ed.), *Encyclopaedia of evaluation* (pp. 376–379). Thousand Oaks: Sage.

Su, F., & Wood, M. (2017). *Cosmopolitan perspectives on academic leadership in higher education*. London: Bloomsbury Publishing.

Taylor, K., Durey, A., Mulcock, J., Kickett, M., & Jones, S. (2014). Developing Aboriginal and Torres Strait Islander cultural capabilities in health graduates: a review of the literature. Retrieved from https://www1.health.gov.au.

Terrell, R. D., & Lindsey, R. B. (2008). *Culturally proficient leadership: The personal journey begins within*. Thousand Oaks, California: Corwin Press.

The University of Sydney. *Wingara Mura—Bunga Barrabugu*. Retrieved from https://sydney.edu.au/content/dam/corporate/documents/about-us/values-and-visions/wingara-mura-bunga-barrabugu.pdf.

The University of Sydney. (2016). The University of Sydney 2016–20 Strategic Plan. Retrieved from https://sydney.edu.au/dam/intranet/documents/strategy-and-planning/strategic-plan-2016-20.pdf.

Thompson, S., Forde, T., & Otieno, T. (2017). A sustainable, culturally competent approach to academic leadership. In J. L. Chin, J. E. Trimble, E. Joseph & J. Garcia (Eds.), *Global and culturally diverse leaders and leadership: New dimension and challenges for business, education and society*. Bingley, U.K: Emerald Publishing.

Universities Australia. (2011). National best practice framework for cultural competency in Australian Universities. Retrieved from http://www.indigenousculturalcompetency.edu.au/index.html.

Chapter 4
Deconstructing and Embedding Cultural Competence in Initial Teacher Education: Responding to University Graduate Qualities for Undergraduate Students

Sheelagh Daniels-Mayes

Abstract Graduate qualities, also known as graduate attributes, are a universalising and common feature in universities (Universities Australia, 2011). The intention is for graduate qualities to be addressed throughout an institution's curricula across all disciplines. Arguably, cultural competence is one of the most value-laden of all graduate qualities, having its origins in the fields of health, human services and education where various frameworks have been developed. The terms 'culture' and 'competence', which are derived from the concept, are complex ideas with no consensus on either term. This paper will focus specifically on the challenges of developing curricular that seeks to embed the graduate quality of 'cultural competence' into a first-year, mandatory Initial Teacher Education (ITE) Unit of Study with a large student cohort. The paper illustrates how the term 'cultural competence' was deconstructed using concept mapping and analysis by a team of diverse teacher educators. While an agreed-upon singular definition of cultural competence was not reached, all team members agreed that cultural competence is a social justice imperative in education. The intent of this paper is not to provide a formulaic, one-size-fits-all approach but rather reflect upon the multi-layered and complex nature of the task of building a future teacher workforce that is engaging in the continuous process of becoming culturally competent in an ever-increasing diverse world.

Keywords Aboriginal · Concept mapping · Cultural competence · Graduate qualities · Initial teacher education

S. Daniels-Mayes (✉)
Sydney School of Education and Social Work, The University of Sydney, Sydney, NSW, Australia
e-mail: sheelagh.daniels-mayes@sydney.edu.au

© The Author(s) 2020

J. Frawley et al. (eds.), *Transforming Lives and Systems*,
SpringerBriefs in Education, https://doi.org/10.1007/978-981-15-5351-6_4

Introduction

Graduate qualities, also known as graduate attributes, are a universalising and common feature in Australian universities (Universities Australia, 2011). The intention is for the graduate qualities to be addressed throughout the institution's curricula across all disciplines. The University of Sydney's 2016–20 Strategic Plan identifies the need to transform the undergraduate curriculum in order to produce graduates with the capacity to influence and contribute to changing and globalised environments (University of Sydney, 2016). The aim of the new curriculum framework is to balance depth of disciplinary expertise with broader capabilities. Nine graduate qualities were identified: depth of disciplinary expertise; critical thinking and problem solving; oral and written communication; information and digital literacy; inventiveness; cultural competence; interdisciplinary effectiveness; integrated professional, ethical and personal identity; and influence (https://sydney.edu.au/students/graduate-qualities.html). One initiative offered by the strategy as a measure of success, states: 'Embed new graduate qualities and a new curriculum framework in all undergraduate qualities' (University of Sydney, 2016, p. 57). The Strategy further states:

> 5.1 Develop interactive and collaborative learning designs that foster excellence and innovation design experiences that promote the alignment of learning and assessment at multiple levels (task, unit, major, degree) and across disciplines.
>
> 5.2 Create contemporary environments that enable flexible and interactive learning (The University of Sydney, 2016, p. 38).

Arguably, cultural competence is one of the most value-laden of all graduate qualities. Cultural competence emerged from the fields of health, human services and education with various frameworks being developed using a diversity of definitions based on their respective disciplinary knowledges and worldviews. My aim in this paper is not to reproduce the extensive body of literature pertaining to cultural competence but rather to highlight the challenges we encountered in this project, starting with defining the term itself. Cross, Bazron, Dennis and Isaacs (1989, p. 189) provide one of the earliest definitions of cultural competence:

> a set of congruent behaviours, attitudes, and policies that come together in a system, agency or among professionals and enable that system, or agency to work effectively in cross-cultural situations.

Used primarily within the health care field, Cross et al. (1989) advocate for cultural competence as a process that exists on a six-component continuum, with cultural destructiveness located at one end and cultural proficiency placed at the opposite end. Within this continuum, cultural competence is situated as the fifth component (Cross, et al., 1989); however, I agree with Davis (2007, p. 35) who argues:

> One may say that even attempting to ascribe a static definition to cultural competence is antithetical to the fluid character fundamental to the concept because what is culturally competent to one may not reflect critical elements important to another.

Perhaps then we need to look at the meaning of the two terms themselves: 'cultural' and 'competence'. First, 'cultural', a derivative of culture, is the adjectival component of the concept. Cross et al. (1989, p.7) define this problematic term as being,

the integrated pattern of human behaviour that includes thoughts, communications, actions, customs, beliefs, values, and institutions of a racial, ethnic, religious, or social group.

Second, 'competence' refers to performance that is sufficient and adequate, with synonyms for competence including capability, skill, fitness, aptitude and expertise (Rosenjack-Burchum, 2002, p. 6). Additionally, a variety of terms exist including cultural awareness, cultural sensitivity, cultural appropriateness, cultural competence, cultural responsiveness, cultural proficiency, cultural understanding, cultural integrity, cultural relevance, cultural humility and cultural safety. In short, the concept of cultural competency is dynamic, evolving and open to interpretation.

Despite the absence of a singularly agreed-upon definition or term, there is one significant theme strongly present in the literature. That is, cultural competence is a social justice project (Andersen, Bunda, & Walter, 2008). With regards to the profession of teaching, Russo (2004) teaching for social justice has two key concepts. First, educators need to be able to recognise cycles of oppression where some groups of people are consistently privileged while others are consistently disadvantaged; the privileging and disadvantaging becomes unjust when it is unearned or undeserved. Second, educators need to become change agents able to interrupt cycles of oppression in their classrooms and the wider educational landscape. Teaching pre-service teachers to know how to disrupt (or challenge) oppression which means learning about (or creating) strategies to counter oppression (of 'race', class, gender, (dis)ability, sexuality and others) across the grade levels and content areas in which our teachers work. Teachers can work as change agents through the content or topics they address as well as through particular pedagogical practices that tend to undermine patterns of entrenched oppression (Russo, 2004). As will be expanded upon below, the imperative of graduating as culturally competent and socially-just teachers was common for all team members. This paper focuses on the processes undertaken to deconstruct the concept of cultural competence and how we embedded the identified components into the chosen course.

Project Overview and Contextualisation

Universities Australia (2011) in collaboration with the Indigenous Higher Education Advisory Council (IHEAC) provided the Australian higher education sector with a best practice framework outlining theoretical and practical tools to embed cultural competence at institutional levels. The objective was to provide encouraging and supportive environments for Indigenous students and staff, as well as to embed for non-Indigenous graduates the knowledge and skills necessary for them to provide genuinely competent services to the Australian Indigenous communities (Universities Australia, 2011, p. 6). In the Australian higher education context, it is considered that a culturally competent university would embrace the following values throughout their organisational fabric and extend cultural competence to every staff member and student. University Australia defines cultural competence in relation to the Australian higher education sector as:

> Student and staff knowledge and understanding of Indigenous Australian cultures, histories and contemporary realities and awareness of Indigenous protocols, combined with the proficiency to engage and work effectively in Indigenous contexts congruent to the expectations of Indigenous Australian peoples (Universities Australia, 2011, p. 6).

Universities Australia (2011, p. 6) goes on to say:

> Indigenous cultural competence requires an organisational culture which is committed to social justice, human rights and the process of reconciliation through valuing and supporting Indigenous cultures, knowledges and peoples as integral to the core business of the institution. It requires effective and inclusive policies and procedures, monitoring mechanisms and allocation of sufficient resources to foster culturally competent behaviour and practice at all levels of the institution.

Overall, University Australia argues that 'all graduates of Australian universities should be culturally competent' (2011, p. 9). More specifically, Recommendation 4 states: 'Train teaching staff in Indigenous pedagogy for teaching Indigenous Studies and students effectively, including developing appropriate content and learning resources, teaching strategies and assessment methods' (University Australia, 2011, p. 9).

Responding to this, funding was received in 2018 for a project named: Incorporating Cultural Competence in Faculty of Education & Social Work Curriculum (Dr. Lynette Riley). This project, which became known as the 'Embeddedness Project', sought to address The University of Sydney's then new graduate quality: To work productively, collaboratively and openly in diverse groups and across cultural boundaries (University of Sydney, 2016, p. 35). The path chosen to achieve this outcome was to initially work with the first-year course coordinators, of the subject *EDUF1018 Education, Teachers and Teaching* (henceforth EDUF1018), which provides an introduction to key concepts in education including pedagogy, curriculum and assessment. This is a mandatory first-year course with a large student cohort of several hundred students in the School of Education and Social Work.

A literature review was undertaken prior to consultation with first-year coordinators that focused on understandings of cultural competence, terminologies used, its key components, frameworks and implementation across different fields and disciplines. Primarily literature from 2000 to the present was considered, though some historical scholarship was reviewed for contextualisation purposes. This revealed a considerable amount of scholarship. However, scant literature on the mechanisms for embedding and assessing cultural competence in university coursework was found. A Google Scholar search for "embed/ding cultural competence" university coursework, found only six hits (Fialho, 2013; Johnson, 2013, 2016; Pace & Blue, 2016; Penn, 2011; Porterfield, 2016) with none of these being of significant help with the project.

The project team consisted of nine teacher educators and a research assistant; members occupied a diversity of marginalised identities including differing cultures, genders, ages, (dis)abilities, and sexual orientations; members traversed the spectrum of early career academics to professorial standing; and while members crossed theoretical boundaries, generally speaking, as noted earlier, members would best be described as being committed to social justice and therefore take a critical stance in their work. As DiAngelo and Sensoy (2014, p. 1) poignantly writes:

> By critical stance we mean those academic fields (including social justice, critical pedagogy, multicultural education, anti-racist, postcolonial, and feminist approaches) that operate from the perspective that knowledge is socially constructed, and that education is a political project embedded within a network of social institutions that reproduce inequality.

We recognised that when people (and in this case first year pre-service teachers) are confronted with evidence of inequality that challenges our identities, the response is often resistance in the form of '…silence, withdrawal, immobilising guilt, feeling overly hopeless or overly hopeful, rejection, anger, sarcasm, and argumentation' (DiAngelo & Sensoy, 2014, p. 1). The often-mainstream narratives that inform our deeply held beliefs make studying and teaching from a critical stance very challenging. Therefore, team members knew that the task of teaching teachers to adopt a critical stance and engage in the process of becoming agents of change (Russo, 2004), is potentially one fraught with difficulty but nonetheless a social justice imperative in an ever-changing, increasingly diverse world. We understood too that graduating students who were all 'culturally competent' was idealistic, and instead aimed to graduate students who would strive to be culturally competent on an ongoing basis, potentially influencing systems, society, schools and education towards achieving social justice (Cross et al., 1989).

Team members met for two hours each week, for eight weeks, and then met as required as EDUF1018 curriculum and assessment was developed. Dropbox Professional was used to share gathered materials. All team members agreed that they did not like the term cultural competence and much discussion ensued. In the end it was decided that as all team members had some familiarity with the term, so cultural competence would be used as a default term (Bennett, Green, Gilbert, & Bessarab, 2013), with the aim of the project being to deconstruct the concept into its relevant components as will now be discussed.

Deconstructing Cultural Competence

While the embeddedness project began with an Aboriginal focus, and kept this central, it evolved to include other categories of difference. Thus, 'cultural competence' came to include (but not limited to): culture, ethnicity, gender, ability, age and underserved communities with Aboriginality remaining central to discussion. This change recognised the multiple and intersecting cultural identities we all occupy. Key to the project was the development of conceptual definitions and teaching resources for explicitly embedding the cultural competence graduate quality in the unit of study for the mandatory subject of EDUF1018.

At the time of inheriting the leadership of this project from Dr Lynette Riley, I worked intuitively, inductively and responsively, drawing on my lived personal and professional experience as an Aboriginal woman living with disability. So, meetings one and two primarily consisted of information-gathering through discussion and brainstorming, gathering project team members' words and phrases to describe cultural competence and any questions or concerns held. This to me, and to team members, was a logical first phase; one that I had used extensively in my professional work as a project manager and researcher. A subsequent literature review revealed the methods of concept mapping (Davis, 2007) and concept analysis (Rodgers, 2000) which well described the approach I had undertaken to deconstruct the concept of cultural competence which I now briefly describe.

First, concept mapping (Davis, 2007) typically consists of six stages: (1) preparing for the project; (2) idea generation; (3) structuring ideas; (4) multivariate analyses; (5) interpretation; and (6) implementation. Second, Rodgers' (2000) concept analysis is understood as an evolutionary and inductive method of analysis, arguing that concepts develop over time and are influenced by the context in which they are used. The embeddedness project combined these two methods and resulted in three phases of the project as follows: (1) the initial phase, which included the collection of scholarship, gathering of team member knowledge and stances; (2) the core analysis and deconstruction and embeddedness process; and (3) the further analysis phase, in which questions for further analysis and work are identified. This project therefore implemented concept mapping and analysis in a way not previously applied to cultural competence and pre-service teacher education. What follows are the overall outcomes of the first two meetings of team members.

Concept Mapping: Meeting One

- Mind map on the whiteboard: priorities, concerns, questions, clarifications.
- No-one liked the term 'cultural competence' but agreed that it was a 'default' term, one that everyone had some familiarity with.
- Need to deconstruct the socially constructed concept of 'cultural competence': conceptual mapping terms.
- Need for future evaluation.
- Ensure the teaching/learning programs are strength based.
- Scaffold teaching and learning for students across all the course so as to decrease student resistance.
- Create consistent resources and definitions for teaching.

Concept Mapping: Meeting Two

Building on Meeting One, team members brainstorm the themes and concepts implied in the term 'cultural competence' (Table 4.1).

Team members sorted generated concepts into conceptual groupings, placing for example, 'deficit and disadvantage', into one concept according to similarities and differences. This brought the deconstructed concepts down from forty-seven components to the twenty-one listed in Table 4.1. It was decided that each concept needed to be expanded upon with: (1) academic definition; (2) everyday definition that first-year students would readily understand; (3) any activities that could be used in lectures or seminars with students; and (4) articles and readings for both students and academics delivering the course. According to team members' knowledge, theoretical framework and lived experience, each member took 'ownership' of one or more concepts and were able to upload and share materials through Dropbox Professional. Each definition was presented to team members for discussion at subsequent meetings, and where need be, clarification was provided. At all times members were mindful of the student cohort to which we were teaching (i.e. first-year education students probably fresh out of high school). What follows (Table 4.2) is one example.

The team recognised that it was not practicable or reasonable for all twenty-one concepts to be included in EDUF1018. Students would, for example, require a scaffolded approach that would provide students with baseline knowledge that could then be built on as their education progressed. It needs to be noted too, that concepts did not necessarily explicitly appear in the unit of study but rather the components were embedded as initially intended. As critical theorists, who understand that knowledge is socially constructed and reinforced by mainstream narratives, we sought to provide a method for students to overcome their resistances and become agents of change in their classrooms and schools. To maximise student's learning of social justice content and subsequent action, our restructuring and course development was guided by the

Table 4.1 Deconstructing cultural competence

Deconstructing cultural competence		
Aboriginality	Equality and equity	Power and privilege
Colonisation and dispossession	Fundamentals (i.e. basic knowledge students should possess)	Racism, 'race' and racialisation
Cultural competence: humility—responsiveness—understanding	Inclusion and Exclusion	Reciprocity
Culturally responsive: schools—teachers—pedagogies	Intersectionality and positionality	Social justice
Culture and cultural	Kinship	Stereotyping
Deficit and disadvantage	Marginalisation and minoritorisation	Subjectivity
Discrimination	Microaggressions	Whiteness

Table 4.2 Microaggressions

Microaggressions	
Definition	Microaggressions are the everyday verbal, nonverbal, and environmental slights, snubs, or insults, whether intentional or unintentional, that communicate hostile, derogatory, or negative messages to target persons based solely upon their marginalized group membership (from Diversity in the Classroom, UCLA Diversity & Faculty Development, 2014). The first step in addressing microaggressions is to recognize when a microaggression has occurred and what message it may be sending. Microaggression: brief, everyday exchanges that send denigrating messages to certain individuals because of their group membership (Wing, 2010).
Resource	Tool: Recognizing microaggressions and the messages they send. Adapted from Wing, D. S. (2010). *Microaggressions in everyday life: Race, gender, and Sexual Orientation.* New Jersey: Wiley
Reading	Fricker (2007). *Epistemic injustice: power and the ethics of knowing.* Oxford: Oxford University Press
Critiques of Microaggression	https://theconversation.com/the-trouble-with-microaggressions-71364 Fricker's (2007) work closely considers the injustice perpetuated and felt by specific individual epistemic practices (e.g., personal processes such as conveying knowledge to others by speech and making meaning of social experiences) within such social contexts. Fricker describes these epistemic injustices as 'testimonial injustice, in which someone is wronged in their capacity as a giver of knowledge; and hermeneutical injustice, in which someone is wronged in their capacity as a subject of social understanding' (page 7).

wisdom of DiAngelo and Sensoy's paper (2014, p. 3) *Leaning in: A student's guide to engaging constructively with social justice content*:

1. Strive for intellectual humility.
2. Recognise the difference between opinions and informed knowledge.
3. Let go of personal anecdotal evidence and look at broader societal patterns.
4. Notice your own defensive reactions and attempt to use these reactions as entry points for gaining deeper self-knowledge.
5. Recognise how your own social positionality (such as your 'race', class, gender, sexuality, ability-status) informs your perspectives and reactions to your instructor and those whose work you study in the course.

If our students could commence their journey down this intellectual and emotional path, then we believed we were on the right track for students to engage in a process of becoming 'culturally competent' teachers upon graduation, and to continue this developmental process beyond university striving for social justice by taking a critical stance (Cross et al., 1989; DiAngelo & Sensoy, 2014).

Implementation of Revised EDUF1018 Unit of Study

In 2018, first-year pre-service students undertook the restructured and revised curriculum that sought to embed cultural competence into the unit of study course. During the twelve-week semester, more time was given to tutorials than to lectures (reduced to one per week in 2018 compared to two one-hour lectures in 2017). Lecture topics and readings reflected the deconstructed cultural competence terms as well as assessment tasks such as weekly self-reflection and groupwork.

Conclusions and Future Directions

The process undertaken in the *Embeddedness Project* needs to be evaluated. So far as we can ascertain from existing publications, *EDUF 1018 Education, Teachers and Teaching* is the first unit of study at the University of Sydney to attempt to embed and assess cultural competence content in response to the new graduate qualities. The first of these subjects EDUF1018 is the unit under restructure here. The key research question is: *How might Cultural Competence content be embedded and assessed effectively whilst not being the core focus of a unit of work?* Indeed, the answer to this question is more widely pressing as there seems to be scant scholarship on the mechanisms for embedding and assessing cultural competence in university coursework generally. In this sense, this research design is more exploratory, rather than confirmatory.

The consultation process in this project relied on teacher educators who possessed a diversity of knowledge and experience who take a critical stance in their teaching and research and are constantly striving to be culturally competent in the situations they find themselves. We believe we've conscientiously embedded the graduate quality cultural competence content in EDUF1018 coursework and assessment, but is this effective from a students' perspective and experience? Is the 'embedding' clear enough for student learning or does it need to be more explicit? If so, what content might that replace? Is there a case that first-year subjects like EDUF1018 are already overloaded with other embeddings such as first year transition and study skills concerns (see for example Gale & Parker, 2014)? Are multiple embeddings overwhelming, distracting or helpful? We recognise that these are not questions that are answerable in the normal teaching and learning cycle or Unit of Study. In-depth exploratory, scholarly analysis of the teaching and learning in EDUF1018 is needed to come to better understand these intersections between embedding 'additional' course content, student learning and developing graduate qualities. While we have begun the process of evaluating the effectiveness of the project, the findings are still under analysis.

Acknowledgements The author acknowledges the project team members, pivotal in the *Embeddedness Project:* Lyn Riley, Tracey Cameron, Samantha McMahon, Matthew Thomas, Remy Low, Vic Rawlings, Alexandra McCormick, Valerie Harwood, Deb Hayes. Additionally, she acknowledges the input of: Belinda Chambers, James Tognolini, Arlene Harvey, Michelle Davidson, David Evans, Mareese Terare, and Jack Frawley, who have driven the Graduate Qualities measuring project of which she has been involved.

References

Andersen, C., Bunda, T., & Walter, M. (2008). Indigenous higher education: The role of universities in releasing the potential. *Australian Journal of Indigenous Education, 37,* 1–8.

Bennett, B., Green, S., Gilbert, S., & Bessarab, D. (2013). *Our voices: Aboriginal and Torres Strait Islander social work.* Melbourne: Palgrave Macmillan.

Cross, T., Bazron, B., Dennis, K., & Isaacs, M. (1989). Towards a culturally competent system of care, vol. 1. Washington. DC: National Technical Assistance Center for Children's Mental Health, Georgetown University Child Development Center.

Davis, T. S. (2007). Mapping patterns of perceptions: A community-based approach to cultural competence assessment. *Research on Social Work Practice, 17*(3), 358–379.

DiAngelo, R., & Sensoy, Ö. (2014). Leaning in: A student's guide to engaging constructively with social justice content. *Radical Pedagogy, 11*(1), (Article 2).

Fialho, M. (2013). *Engage, Empower, enact: Evaluating a cultural competence program at UWA.* Perth, WA: University of Western Australia.

Fricker, M. (2007). *Epistemic injustice: Power and the ethics of knowing.* Oxford: Oxford University Press.

Gale, T., & Parker, S. (2014). Navigating change: A typology of student transition in higher education. *Studies in Higher Education, 39*(5), 734–753. https://doi.org/10.1080/03075079.2012. 721351.

Johnson, J. L. (2013) School psychology and cultural responsiveness: Re-forming identities. PhD Thesis: University of Missouri-St. Louis.

Johnson, T. M. (2016). Culturally responsive policy in an urban Head Start program. Doctoral Dissertations. National Louis University, Dissertation Paper 163.

Pace, D. A., & Blue, E. V. (2016). Meeting the international need for special educators with online education. *Journal of the International Association of Special Education, 1,* 100–108.

Penn, C. (2011). Cultural safety and the curriculum: Recommendations for global practice. *Perspectives on Global Issues in Communication Sciences and Related Disorders, 1,* 4–11. https://doi.org/10.1044/gics1.1.4.

Porterfield, M. L. (2016). Cultural competence in North Carolina's early care and education system. Master's Thesis. University of North Carolina, Greensboro.

Rodgers, B. L. (2000). Concept analysis: An evolutionary view. In B. L. Rodgers & K. A. Knafl (Eds.), *Concept development in nursing: Foundations, techniques, and applications* (pp. 77–102). Philadelphia: Saunders.

Rosenjack-Burchum, J. L. (2002). Cultural competence: An evolutionary perspective. *Nursing Forum, 37*(4), 5–15.

Russo, P. (2004). What does it mean to teach for social justice? Retrieved from https://www.oswego. edu/~prusso1/Russos_what_does_it_mean_to_teach_for_s.htm.

The University of Sydney. (2016). *The University of Sydney 2016–20 Strategic Plan*. Retrieved from https://sydney.edu.au/dam/intranet/documents/strategy-and-planning/strategic-plan-2016-20.pdf.

Universities Australia. (2011). *National best practice framework for cultural competency in Australian Universities*. Retrieved from http://www.indigenousculturalcompetency.edu.au/index.html.

Wing, D. S. (2010). *Microaggressions in everyday life: Race, gender, and Sexual Orientation*. New Jersey: Wiley, New Jersey.

Chapter 5
Navigating the Cultural Interface to Develop a Model for Dentistry Education: Cultural Competence Curricula in Dentistry Education

Cathryn Forsyth, Stephanie D. Short, Michelle Irving, Marc Tennant, and John Gilroy

Abstract Indigenous people in Australia experience a greater burden of dental and oral disease than non-Indigenous Australians. Cultural competence of the dental team is crucial in the delivery of oral health services in addressing these health disparities. Higher education institutions across Australia are required to incorporate Indigenous culture into their curricula to improve educational outcomes for Indigenous peoples and to increase cultural competence of staff and students. A research team of Indigenous and non-Indigenous oral health, dental and social science researchers conducted a comprehensive four-phase case study to identify cultural competence curriculum interventions in dentistry education, provide a baseline investigation of Indigenous cultural competence curricula practices and ascertain barriers and enablers to integrating Indigenous cultural competence into dentistry programmes. The culmination of this research has resulted in the development of an Indigenous cultural competence model to assist dental education within Australian. Our research team established a Cultural Competence Curriculum Review Reference Group comprising Indigenous and non-Indigenous members. Indigenous and non-Indigenous research team and reference group members are engaged within the cultural interface at each phase of this research to facilitate culturally safe research practices and ensure authentication and validity of the data. The process of how we developed this model and the relationships built during this research is the focus of this chapter. How do Indigenous and non-Indigenous researchers work together to achieve positive outcomes?

Keywords Culture · Education · Dental · Oral health · Indigenous · Australia

C. Forsyth (✉) · M. Irving
School of Dentistry, The University of Sydney, Sydney, NSW, Australia
e-mail: Cathryn.Forsyth@sydney.edu.au

S. D. Short · J. Gilroy
Faculty of Medicine and Health, The University of Sydney, Sydney, NSW, Australia

M. Tennant
International Research Collaborative, Oral Health and Equity, The University of Western Australia, Perth, Australia

J. Frawley et al. (eds.), *Transforming Lives and Systems*,
SpringerBriefs in Education, https://doi.org/10.1007/978-981-15-5351-6_5

Background

Indigenous peoples within Australia experience higher mortality rates and carry the greatest burden of disease in terms of both general and oral health. Several closing-the-gap policies have failed to achieve significant improvements in health outcomes. Unacceptable disparities in health and disease continue to exist, leaving Indigenous Australians disadvantaged across a range of health indicators (Vos, Barker, & Begg, 2009; Mitrou, Cook, & Lawrence, 2014).

Several higher education reviews have identified the need for all tertiary institutions to incorporate Indigenous culture and knowledge more widely into all faculty curricula to improve educational outcomes for Indigenous Australians and to increase cultural competence among all students. In 2008, the Bradley 'Review of Australian Higher Education' recommended that higher education providers should ensure that the institutional culture, the cultural competence of staff and the nature of the curriculum recognise and support the participation of Indigenous students and that Indigenous knowledge should be embedded into the curriculum so that all students gain an understanding of Indigenous culture (Bradley, Noonan, Nugent, & Scales, 2008). Universities Australia investigated existing Indigenous cultural competency initiatives and programmes in Australian universities to establish a clear baseline for Indigenous cultural competency activities. Subsequently, a *National Best Practice Framework and Guiding Principles for Indigenous Cultural Competency in Australian Universities* was developed (Universities Australia, 2011a, b). During 2012, the *Behrendt Review of Higher Education Access and Outcomes for Aboriginal and Torres Strait Islander People*, building on the Bradley Review, examined how improving higher education outcomes among Indigenous people would contribute to nation-building and reduce Indigenous disadvantage (Behrendt, Larkin, Griew, & Kelly, 2012).

An Indigenous cultural competence curriculum framework for dental students was developed in 2007 by a team at the Centre for Rural and Remote Oral Health, and now the IRCOHE at the University of Western Australia (Bazen, Paul, & Tennant, 2007). As the accreditation standards for dental schools at that time did not include mandatory Indigenous cultural curricula, the changes were not maintained. However, recent accreditation standards by the Australian Dental Council require all dentistry and oral health professionals within Australia to provide culturally safe and culturally competent practice that includes recognition of the distinct needs of Indigenous Australians in relation to oral healthcare provision (ADC, 2016).

As cultural competence gains momentum and is linked to regulatory and accreditation processes, it will be essential to develop nationally standardised educational programmes based on a unified conceptual teaching framework. In higher education, academics will be required to consider how best to train the future healthcare workforce, and cultural competence training for faculty members will be crucial to achieving research outcomes on cultural competence interventions (Bainbridge, McCalman, Clifford, & Tsey, 2015). Indigenous people in Australia are significantly under-represented in the higher education and healthcare systems, which contributes to the high levels of social and economic disadvantage they often experience. Producing Indigenous graduates who are qualified to take up professional, academic and leadership positions within community, government and corporate sectors will help to address this disadvantage (Behrendt et al., 2012).

The Indigenous concept of health is holistic, with self-determination being central to the provision of Indigenous health services (Durie, 2014). A culturally valid understanding must shape provision of Indigenous healthcare, acknowledging experiences of trauma and loss have greatly contributed to the impairment of Indigenous culture, health and well-being (Dury & Thompson, 2012). Recognition of existing colonial ways, power imbalances and dominant or oppressive policies within the healthcare system will aid in understanding Indigenous perspectives.

University curricula, teaching methodologies and research endeavours have a history of development that contributed to the dispossession of Indigenous people (Martin, 2003; Moreton-Robinson, Casey, & Nicoll, 2008). Historical foundations of dentistry and oral health education and research in Australia have been developed in accordance with Western epistemology. Non-Indigenous researchers have considered Indigenous knowledge as second-rate describing themselves as the producers of knowledge (Moreton-Robinson, 2004). Medical, health and social sciences within Universities have focused on modern and industrialised concepts based on assumptions about the superiority of Western culture (Connell, 2007). Educational institutions, healthcare services and government departments have been established within colonial traditions, overtly and covertly supporting power, privilege and continuation of colonial ways. Indigenous peoples are often viewed as being problematic and costly, with media and history books providing Eurocentric viewpoints, consequently resulting in oppression and continuation of poor health outcomes (Moreton-Robinson, 2004, 2008; Sherwood, 2009). It is paramount that Indigenous people are active participants in any Indigenous research, as Indigenous people have a level of experience and knowledge of colonisation and dispossession that a non-Indigenous person could not obtain (Tuhiwai-Smith, 1999; Esgin, Hersh, Rowley, Gilroy, & Newton, 2018).

Complex issues surround the concept of cultural competence and the acute need for health practitioners to develop knowledge, skills, understandings and attributes to be responsive in diverse cultural settings. The human rights of Indigenous people must be recognised and enforced, with racism, adversity, stigma and social disadvantage, being addressed in strategies aimed at improving Indigenous health. The centrality and strength of Indigenous family and kinship must be understood, along with diversity of Indigenous people groups being recognised. We need to move beyond the traditional biomedical model of healthcare and embrace a holistic model of care encompassing a more culturally responsive, client-centred, holistic model of care (Dudgeon, Milroy, & Walker, 2014).

Reflective practice is a major tool used within professional disciplines to assist in developing appropriate client–practitioner relationships, and encouraging practitioners to explore uncertainties and difficulties in our sense-making, to identify inconsistencies between what we think and what we do (Fook & Gardner, 2007).

Reflective practice encourages us to compare our current practices with new experiences, developing a deeper understanding of issues, motivating us to change over time (Prochaska, 1997). Critical self-reflection is a useful decolonising tool as it assists in questioning our assumptions, challenges our values and beliefs, and identifies individual and institutional practices that perpetuate racism and injustice (Harvey & Russell-Mundine, 2019). In the next section we will explore how our team utilised Indigenous methodologies within our research, and in the final section our first author will share some reflections of her experiences in navigating this cultural interface.

Use of Indigenous Methodologies Within Research

A methodology that was appropriate for Indigenous people was designed with a working group that consisted of Indigenous Elders, Indigenous scholars and non-Indigenous scholars for this case study. Current frameworks in dental sciences were not appropriate for this case study as they fail to acknowledge the diversity within Indigenous lands and cultures and maintain dominant colonial ways. Employing Indigenous decolonisation methodologies provides a better understanding of particular motivations and behaviours within Indigenous communities, unearthing aspects which have not been previously explored. Each Indigenous community must be understood in the context of their experience of colonisation, disadvantage and cultural heritage (Gilroy, Donelly, Colmar, & Parmenter, 2013).

Reflecting Indigenous methodologies, an Indigenous research governance model was employed, with this research team establishing a Cultural Competence Curriculum Review Reference Group in mid-2015, comprising Indigenous and non-Indigenous scholars and leaders. Collaborations between the reference group and our Indigenous and non-Indigenous dental, oral health and social scientific research team were ongoing. During development of the ethics application, our reference group was involved to ensure all researches conducted were in keeping with the National Health and Medical Research Council Guidelines (NHMRC, 2003, 2013). At each phase of data collection and analysis, the reference group and research team met to discuss research findings, supporting verification of all data and maximising authenticity of all data. Indigenous methodologies informed this entire research process.

Three fundamental principles were adopted when conducting this research. First, this research was counter-hegemonic to Western ideologies, strengthening and supporting the fight to alleviate social conditions that result in poor quality of life for Indigenous people. Secondly, this research privileged the Indigenous voice to depict various experiences of Indigenous people and ensure non-Indigenous populations are aware of the concerns and ambitions of Indigenous spokespeople. Thirdly, this research was conducted by Indigenous and non-Indigenous researchers (Foley, 2006; Rigney, 1999). The third point reinforces the notion that Indigenous people have a level of knowledge and experience that non-Indigenous researchers could not possibly acquire; hence Indigenous people need to be explicitly involved in any Indigenous research. Gilroy, an Indigenous sociologist, developed criteria for use in working with Indigenous peoples with disabilities. These criteria assisted researchers and policy advisors to develop research for and with Indigenous people with disabilities (Gilroy et al., 2013).

Indigenous methodologies identify power imbalances that have existed since colonisation and examine dominant and oppressive policy. Indigenous methodologies deconstruct myths or particular practices and respect Indigenous ways of knowing, being and doing, providing balanced views about Indigenous people's circumstances (Ganesharajah, 2009; Martin, 2003; Sherwood, 2009, 2013). Although many Indigenous elders and community members have participated actively in voicing their concerns about social justice and health issues, power differentials continue to exist resulting in the continuation of poor policy and service provision for Indigenous people. Indigenous people need to share their stories and provide an Indigenous perspective on social and health issues, to facilitate improvement in the health and wellbeing of Indigenous people (Sherwood, 2006).

This research team acknowledges other research methods used globally that are consistent with Indigenous methodologies such as Participatory Action Research (PAR) and Community Based Participatory Research (CBPR). PAR involves inquiry, reflection and action that aim to improve health and reduce health inequalities by embracing methodological approaches to hand over power from the researcher to the research participants. PAR complements the principles held by academic researchers in the fields of anthropology, social sciences, theology and community development (Bennett, 2004; Baum, MacDougall, & Smith, 2006). CBPR integrates education and social action to improve health and reduce health disparities, focusing on building relationships between academics and community partners, through a long-term commitment, active participation and learning together in a spirit of reciprocity. Similar to Indigenous methodologies, CBPR challenges mutuality of the research relationship, especially around issues of power, privilege, community consent, racial discrimination and the role of research in affirmative social change (Wallerstein et al., 2006, 2010).

Our research team integrated Gilroy's criteria (Gilroy et al., 2013) throughout this research emphasising the importance of including Indigenous community within the research team to ensure equal distribution of power and responsibility. Colonisation has been recognised as a social determinant of health, with the research team being well-informed of colonial influences and the historical dispossession of Indigenous land, traditions and culture (Sherwood, 2013). Similarities and differences between Indigenous communities and understanding struggles faced by Indigenous communities to attain rights to be self-sustaining have been acknowledged. Indigenous and non-Indigenous research team members have met in this cultural interface, gaining a profound understanding of the issues at hand from each other. Together these criteria have empowered our Indigenous researcher and reference group members, improving relationships between Indigenous and non-Indigenous researchers.

Within this methodological framework the case study was conducted in four phases: First, a systematic search of the literature was undertaken in 2016 to identify studies on cultural competence curriculum interventions in dentistry and oral health higher education. Qualitative analysis was undertaken to explore in detail participants personal and educational experiences with cultural competence curricula (Forsyth, Irving, Tennant, Short, & Gilroy, 2017a). Secondly, a survey involving all staff and students of the Doctor of Dental Medicine (DMD) and Bachelor of Oral Health (BOH) programs at the University of Sydney was conducted during 2017, to gather a snapshot of current Indigenous curricula practices in the respective courses (Forsyth et al., 2017b). Thirdly, all School of Dentistry academics and students from the DMD and BOH programmes were invited to participate in in-depth interviews to determine barriers and enablers to integrating Indigenous culture into dentistry and oral health curricula throughout 2018. Thematic analysis was performed using deductive and inductive processes. Our reference group collaborated at each phase of this research to discuss formulation of codes and themes and make sense of the data (Forsyth et al., 2018, 2019). Fourthly, an Indigenous cultural curriculum model was developed in 2019 to assist in the integration of Indigenous curricula for all dental and oral health schools in Australia. Effective Indigenous cultural curricula in dentistry and oral health education will facilitate an improvement in the delivery of oral health services to Australia's Indigenous peoples and have a positive impact on the general health of Australian Indigenous peoples.

Indigenous people are entwined within this much contested knowledge space referred to as the 'cultural interface' (Nakata, 2004). This cultural interface is the sphere where two different histories, cultures, philosophies and practices intersect, creating environments that influence the way Indigenous peoples make sense of and participate in society. As Indigenous and non-Indigenous people socialise within this interface, a greater level of understanding of Indigenous issues result; however as there are so many conflicting and competing discourses that distinguish traditional from non-traditional, this interface will always be distorted. The theory of the cultural interface illuminates difficulties in sharing and interpreting knowledge between Indigenous and non-Indigenous people. This is often due to a focus on difference rather than facilitating an understanding of the meaning of knowledges from both sides. Examining differences between cultural groups ignores the existence of the cultural interface as it does not deconstruct Western epistemologies; rather it upholds Indigenous people as helpless victims of colonisation and establishes power relationships in favour of non-Indigenous people. The theory of the cultural interface requires breaking away from 'us' and 'them' and critiquing how interactions at the cultural interface reinforce non-Indigenous culture as dominant in the Australian political system and hence in the healthcare system. Indigenous people distrust institutions managed by non-Indigenous people due to past experiences of forced removal of children and Indigenous assimilation policies (Nakata, 2004).

Personal Reflection of First Author

As a non-Indigenous clinician and researcher, my Indigenous cultural competency journey commenced as a child with my Indigenous friend in primary school, who was adopted by a non-Indigenous family in the early 1970s. Our families spent time together outside of school. I learnt several years later that my friend had attempted to reconnect with her Indigenous family and struggled for several years before passing away. This greatly affected me and prompted many questions. It was not until I commenced work at the University of Sydney in 2005 that I was provided with this unique opportunity to work alongside Indigenous academics and professional staff and learn more about the difficulties my friend would have experienced.

Whilst attending an Indigenous Oral Health Conference at Uluru in remote Central Australia in 2005, I became more acutely aware of the significant disadvantages experienced by Indigenous Australians. Following this conference, I reflected on what we can do differently within Sydney Dental School to address this oral health disadvantage. Consequently, I built relationships with local Indigenous health workers to form partnerships for future student oral health prevention and health promotion projects. Initial engagement with the Mt Druitt Aboriginal Health Unit was helpful in developing the inaugural Bachelor of Oral Health (BOH) student project in 2007. I was invited to attend several Sorry Day events with this Unit, and my undergraduate students have been involved in numerous celebrations organised by the National Aborigines and Islanders Day Observance Committee (NAIDOC), with student oral health projects continuing to this day. During this time, I continued to reflect on my own experiences, realising how much my life has been one of power and privilege. I appreciated hearing the stories of my Indigenous colleagues and continued to grow in my understanding of why health and education disparities still exist. My knowledge and attitudes were changing and as a result of these relationships, I was able to establish my Indigenous Reference Group for this research project, as described below.

Throughout 2009–10, I completed my Master of Education in Higher Education and Research Methodology. During this time, I had the welcome opportunity to conduct a higher education research project with two Indigenous academics, Dr. John Evans and Dr Katrina Thorpe. This not only increased my understanding of qualitative research methods, but allowed me to share life with two capable and active Indigenous academics. My first Indigenous BOH student commenced in 2009 and completed an oral health promotion programme with Indigenous 'Mums and Bubs' in Albury prior to graduating in 2012. This inaugural BOH program generated greater understanding of Indigenous culture for me and facilitated opportunities to develop additional oral health promotion programs for future BOH students within Indigenous communities.

A Kinship Workshop facilitated by Dr Lynette Riley, a Wiradjuri and Gamilaroi woman and academic at the University of Sydney, was conducted in 2012. My involvement in this workshop not only increased my knowledge and understanding of Aboriginal history and culture but was instrumental in forming relationships with other University of Sydney academics, who were either Indigenous or people with an interest in Indigenous issues. I am still in regular contact with many whom I met at this workshop.

Since 2013, I have valued working with various Indigenous teams across the university, each with different perspectives. The Poche Centre for Indigenous Health has collaborated with the Sydney Dental School to develop a comprehensive oral health programme in the Central Tablelands region of New South Wales. I have been privileged to liaise with Poche team members in the University of Sydney as well as conduct field trips to the Central Tablelands in preparation for Bachelor of Oral Health (BOH) and Doctor of Dental Medicine (DMD) student programs. It is through this collaboration and local contact with Blacktown Department of Technical and Further Education and the Mana Yura student support services that an effective Indigenous student recruitment and retention policy for the BOH and DMD programs was developed. As a result, we have had another three Indigenous students complete the BOH program and another two Indigenous students are currently enrolled in the BOH program. My first Indigenous BOH graduate has been employed as a part-time clinical educator over the past three years and I have had the privilege of supervising her to completion of her Master of Education in 2017. This student is now preparing to commence the Doctor of Dentistry program in 2020.

I have also had the privilege of working with the Wingara Mura Bunga Barrabugu Indigenous strategy team, led by the Deputy Vice Chancellor (Indigenous Strategy and Service) at the University of Sydney. This has involved Indigenous camps and day programmes run by the Widening Participation unit throughout the University calendar year to provide opportunity for Indigenous school students to experience university life. Furthermore, the National Centre for Cultural Competence (NCCC) at the University of Sydney conducted a leadership training programme at Murramarang National Park, which provided an excellent opportunity to be immersed in Indigenous culture and form relationships with other academic and professional staff within the University. I have been involved in regular network meetings and include online modules developed by the NCCC in dental and oral health curricula (Sherwood & Russell-Mundine, 2017).

Sharing in conversations with Indigenous academics, professional staff and students over several years has helped me to understand the importance of self-determination for Indigenous peoples. In the past, my historical understanding of Australia has been presented to me through the eyes of colonists. It is only as Indigenous colleagues are able to voice their concerns and present history from their perspective that we can truly work within this cultural interface and achieve reconciliation.

Following the appointment of my 'Dream Team', John Gilroy and I met to discuss the formation of an Indigenous Reference Group with Indigenous and non-Indigenous participants. As I had ongoing contact with local Indigenous community health professionals, I invited two of these—my BOH Indigenous graduate and a non-Indigenous DMD clinical educator—to join this reference group to meet twice each year. During reference group meetings, I learnt much about the effects of colonisation on Indigenous Australians and how many policies and actions are based on colonial ways. Additionally, I learnt how to approach meetings in a more culturally sensitive manner and identified my own cultural stereotypes and biases. Throughout reference group meetings, I presented findings from each phase of my research and gained significant insight as we viewed these from an Indigenous perspective.

Despite good intentions, there have been many occasions on which the non-Indigenous members of the research team have learnt from our Indigenous researcher and Cultural Competence Curriculum Review Reference Group members. At our first Cultural Competence Curriculum Review Reference Group meeting in 2015, I attempted to be culturally sensitive, welcoming members on arrival and arranging the seating in a circle. Although I knew each person in the meeting, I was aware others had not yet met, so I asked them to introduce themselves before asking our eldest Indigenous member to acknowledge country. When it came turn for our eldest Indigenous member to introduce herself, she stopped, mentioned the correct protocol for acknowledging country before any introductions, and acknowledged country before proceeding with the meeting agenda. On another occasion, when our team was starting to analyse data from the student in-depth interviews, our Indigenous researcher, Dr John Gilroy, randomly selected a few to analyse and found considerable use of the language of 'us' and 'them' throughout the interviews. Initially, I and other non-Indigenous members of the team did not recognise the use of such language. It was not until our Indigenous sociologist brought this to our attention that we were able to recognise the use of such language and gain insight into its historical use by the dominant western culture.

In the final phase of this research, I was attempting to incorporate how we utilised Indigenous methodologies as the conceptual framework for the entire case study. Although I thought I had done a reasonable job of including Indigenous methodologies content in my thesis, it was not until John Gilroy had a long discussion with me and suggested further reading that I understood I had not fully expressed this and that I lacked evidence of my research process. It was during this time of deliberation and reflection that I realised the extent to which my research team and reference group were intertwined in an Indigenous and non-Indigenous cultural interface, building bridges between Indigenous and non-Indigenous academics and healthcare workers, gaining greater understanding of each other and responding to challenges that emerged.

As a result of my research journey, I have gained much insight into historical and contemporary power differentials, privilege position and racism that have impacted upon the health and wellbeing of Indigenous Australians. It is only as Indigenous and non-Indigenous researchers and community members work together, that a greater understanding of Indigenous ways of knowing, being and doing can be understood, empowering the Indigenous voice, to ensure all research endeavours result in positive outcomes for Indigenous peoples.

In May 2019 Professor Heiko Spallek, my Dean, asked if I could prepare a response to the Australian Health Practitioners Regulation Agency (AHPRA) consultation on the definition of cultural safety on behalf of Sydney Dental School. As a result of my research experiences, I was able to develop an initial response to send to the Deputy Vice Chancellor (Indigenous Strategy and Services) and Associate Dean (Indigenous Strategy and Services) Faculty of Medicine and Health, for their feedback. After reflecting on their feedback my response was warmly received. This was a valuable learning experience in utilising my growing knowledge of Indigenous cultural competence in dentistry education and translating this knowledge into other contexts. Building positive professional relationships has been vital in navigating the cultural interface as a non-Indigenous person. I intend to use these positive relationships to pave the way for necessary change within dentistry and oral health education, to improve oral health outcomes for Indigenous Australians and promote reconciliation between Indigenous and non-Indigenous people within Australia.

Conclusion

Indigenous research conducted by Indigenous and non-Indigenous researchers is effective in building positive relationships to navigate the cultural interface. This research team established a Cultural Competence Curriculum Review Reference Group comprising Indigenous and non-Indigenous members. Reference group and research team members collaborated within the cultural interface at each phase of this research resulting in culturally safe research practices and authentication and validity of the data, to develop a model to integrate Indigenous culture into dentistry curricula. As Indigenous and non-Indigenous researchers functioned together to achieve significant research outcomes, a greater respect for one another resulted facilitating reconciliation between Indigenous and non-Indigenous team members. It is imperative that non-Indigenous researchers explicitly involve Indigenous researchers and Indigenous community members in Indigenous research to safeguard power distribution and ensure a culturally safe working environment, to achieve positive research outcomes as Indigenous people have a level of knowledge and experience that non-Indigenous researchers could not possibly acquire.

Acknowledgments The authors acknowledge the invaluable contribution of the Cultural Competence Curriculum Review Reference Group: Linda Lewis, Aboriginal Otitis Media Coordinator, WSLHD; Boe Rambaldini, Director, Poche Centre for Indigenous Health, University of Sydney; Jacinda Stamenkovic, Aboriginal graduate of the Bachelor in Oral Health program and Clinical Educator; Dr Nigel Rock, Doctor of Dental Medicine Clinical Educator, University of Sydney; and Professor Heiko Spallek, Head of School and Dean, Sydney Dental School, University of Sydney. They thank Bettina Fulham, for her dedication as our Research Administrative Assistant.

References

Australian Dental Council. (2016). Professional competencies of the newly qualified dentist. Retrieved from https://www.adc.org.au/sites/default/files/Media_Libraries/PDF/Accreditation/Professional%20Competencies%20of%20the%20Newly%20Qualified%20Dentist_rebrand.pdf.

AHPRA Cultural Safety Consultation. (2019). Retrieved from https://www.ahpra.gov.au/News/2019-04-03-cultural-safety.aspx.

Bainbridge, R., McCalman, J., Clifford, A., & Tsey, K. (2015). *Cultural competency in the delivery of health services for Indigenous people*. Canberra: Closing the Gap Clearinghouse.

Baum, F., MacDougall, C., & Smith, D. (2006). Participatory action research. *Journal of Epidemiology and Community Health, 60*(10), 854–857. https://doi.org/10.1136/jech.2004.028662.

Bazen, J., Paul, D., & Tennant, M. (2007). An Aboriginal and Torres Strait Islander oral health curriculum framework: Development experiences in Western Australia. *Australian Dentist Journal, 52*(2), 86–92.

Behrendt, L., Larkin, S., Griew, R., & Kelly, P. (2012). *Review of higher education access and outcomes for Aboriginal and Torres Strait Islander people final report*. Canberra: AGPS.

Bennett, M. (2004). A review of the literature on the benefits and drawbacks of participatory action research. *First Peoples Child & Family Review, 1*(1), 19–32.

Bradley, D., Noonan, P., Nugent, H., & Scales, B. (2008). *Review of Australian Higher Education Final Report*. Canberra, ACT: Department of Education, Employment and Workplace Relations.

Connell, R. (2007). *Southern Theory: The global dynamics of knowledge in the social sciences*. Crows Nest, NSW: Allen & Unwin.

Dudgeon, P., Milroy, H., & Walker, R. (2014). *Working together: Aboriginal and Torres Strait Islander mental health and wellbeing principles and practice*. Canberra: Commonwealth of Australia.

Durie, M. (2014). Understanding health and illness: research at the interface between science and indigenous knowledge. *International Journal of Epidemiology, 33*, 1138–1143.

Dury, A., & Thompson, S. (2012). Reducing the health disparities of Indigenous Australians: Time to change focus. *BMC Health Services Research, 12*, 151.

Esgin, T., Hersh, D., Rowley, K., Gilroy, J., & Newton, R. (2018). Indigenous research methodologies: decolonizing the Australian sports sciences. *Health promotion international*, https://doi.org/10.1093/heapro/day076.

Foley, D. (2006). Indigenous standpoint theory: An acceptable academic research process for Indigenous academics. *International Journal of the Humanities, 3*(4), 25–36.

Fook, J., & Gardner, F. (2007). *Practising critical reflection: A resource handbook* (p. 2007). Berkshire: Open University Press.

Forsyth, C. J., Irving, M. J., Tennant, M., Short, S. D., & Gilroy, J. A. (2017a). Teaching cultural competence in dental education: A systematic review and exploration of implications for Indigenous populations in Australia. *Journal of Dental Education, 81*, 956–968.

Forsyth, C. J., Irving, M. J., Tennant, M., Short, S. D., & Gilroy, J. A. (2017b). Indigenous cultural competence: A dental faculty curriculum review. *European Journal of Dental Education*, https://doi.org/10.1111/eje.12320.

Forsyth, C. J., Irving, M. J., Short, S. D., Tennant, M., & Gilroy J. A. (2018). Strengthening Indigenous cultural competence in dentistry and oral health education: Academic perspectives. *European Journal of Dental Education*, https://doi.org/10.1111/eje.12398.

Forsyth, C. J., Irving, M. J., Short, S. D., Tennant, M., & Gilroy, J. A. (2019). Students don't know what they don't know: Dental and oral health students' perspectives on developing cultural competence regarding Indigenous peoples. *Journal of Dental Education, 83*(6), 679–686.

Ganesharajah, C. (2009). *Indigenous health and wellbeing: The importance of country*. Canberra, ACT: Australian Institute of Aboriginal and Torres Strait Islander Studies.

Gilroy, J., Donelly, M., Colmar, S., & Parmenter, T. (2013). Conceptual framework for policy and research development with Indigenous people with a disability. *Australian Aboriginal Studies, 2*, 42–58.

Harvey, A., & Russell-Mundine, G. (2019). Decolonising the curriculum: using graduate qualities to embed Indigenous knowledges at the academic cultural interface. *Teaching in Higher Education, 24*(6), 789–808.

Martin, K. (2003). Ways of knowing, ways of being and ways of doing: a theoretical framework and methods for Indigenous research and Indigenist research. *Journal of Australian Studies, 76*, 203–214.

Mitrou, F., Cook, M., & Lawrence, D. (2014). Gaps in Indigenous disadvantage not closing: A census cohort study of social determinants of health in Australia, Canada, & New Zealand from 1981 to 2006. *BMC Public Health, 14*, 201.

Moreton-Robinson, A. (2004). Whiteness, epistemology and Indigenous representation. In A. Moreton-Robinson (Ed.), *Whitening race: Essays in social and cultural criticism* (pp. 75–88). Canberra: Aboriginal Studies Press.

Moreton-Robinson, A., Casey, M., & Nicoll, F. (2008). *Transnational whiteness matters*. Lanham, MD: Lexington Books.

NAIDOC History. (n.d.). Retrieved from https://www.naidoc.org.au/about/history.

Nakata, M. (2004). Indigenous knowledge and the cultural interface: underlying issues at the intersection of knowledge and information systems. *IFLA Journal, 28*(5–6), 281–291.

National Health and Medical Research Council. (2003). *Values and ethics: Guidelines for ethical conduct in Aboriginal and Torres Strait Islander health research.* Canberra: Australian Government Publishing.

National Health and Medical Research Council. (2013). *Guidelines for research into Aboriginal health: Key principles.* Sydney: Aboriginal Health & Medical Research Council of NSW.

Prochaska, J. O., & Velicer, W. F. (1997). The Transtheoretical model of health behavior change. *American Journal of Health Promotion, 12*(1), 38–48.

Riley, L. (n.d.). *Kinship modules.* Retrieved from https://sydney.edu.au/about-us/vision-and-values/our-aboriginal-and-torres-strait-islander-community/kinship-module.html.

Rigney, L. (1999). Internationalisation of an Indigenous anticolonial cultural critique of research methodologies: A guide to Indigenist research methodology and its principles. *Wicazo SA Review,* Autumn, 12.

Sherwood, J., & Edwards, T. (2006). Decolonisation: A critical step for improving Aboriginal health. *Contemporary Nursing, 22,* 178–190.

Sherwood, J. (2009). Who is not coping with colonization? Laying out the map for decolonization. *Australasian Psychiatry,* https://doi.org/10.1080/10398560902948662.

Sherwood, J. (2013). Colonisation—It's bad for your health: The context of Aboriginal health. *Contemporary Nurse, 46*(1), 28–40.

Sherwood, J., & Russell-Mundine, G. (2017). How we do business: Setting the agenda for cultural competence at the University of Sydney. In J. Frawley, S. Larkin, & J. A. Smith (Eds.), *Indigenous pathways, transitions and participation in higher education.* Springer Open: Singapore.

Tuhiwai-Smith, L. (1999). *Decolonising methodologies: Research and Indigenous peoples.* Dunedin: University of Otago Press.

Australia, U. (2011a). *National best practice framework for Indigenous cultural competence.* Canberra, ACT: Universities Australia.

Australia, U. (2011b). *Guiding principles for developing Indigenous cultural competence in Australian universities.* Canberra, ACT: Universities Australia.

Wallerstein, N., & Duran, B. (2006). Using community-based participatory research to address health disparities. *Health Promotion Practice, 7*(3), 312–323. https://doi.org/10.1177/1524839906289376.

Wallerstein, N., & Duran, B. (2010). Community-based participatory research contributions to intervention research: The intersection of science and practice to improve health equity. *American Journal of Public Health,* Supplement 1, *100*(S1).

Vos, T., Barker, B., & Begg, S. (2009). Burden of disease and injury in Aboriginal and Torres Strait Islander people: The Indigenous health gap. *International Journal of Epidemiology, 38,* 470–477.

Chapter 6
Fostering Diversity Competence in the Veterinary Curriculum

Jaime Gongora, Meg Vost, Sanaa Zaki, Stewart Sutherland, and Rosanne Taylor

Abstract The Sydney School of Veterinary Science (SSVS), University of Sydney, recognises the ever-increasing importance of cultural competence (CC) and cultural capacity in professional and research practice and has been working since 2012 on the embedding of CC into the pre-veterinary programmes: Bachelor of Veterinary Biology (BVB) and the Doctor of Veterinary Medicine (DVM). During both their professional lives and while studying, veterinarians work in culturally and linguistically diverse teams and environments. Cultural perspectives can impact animal health, welfare and/or research outcomes and also relationships with communities. It is therefore important to build cultural capacity in graduates and prepare them with relevant skills such as the ability to reflect on cultural belief systems and worldviews present in themselves and in those with whom they interact. To address this, we introduced a broad framework (graduate qualities, learning outcomes and a rubric) that defines CC beyond the context of cultural and linguistic diversity and includes other self-defined cultural groups, and incorporates cultural awareness and competency for working across cultures. We embedded CC vertically into seven units of study within the pre-veterinary BVB and postgraduate DVM programmes. The major areas that were embedded include: Indigenous perceptions and knowledge about animals; principles of cultural competence; effective communication across cultures; and the impact of CC on professional practice, animal management and research. This initiative constitutes a crucial milestone for students and outcomes indicate that students have been inspired to develop core knowledge and skills in this critical area, skills which they will carry with them when approaching extramural rotations in remote communities and overseas, as well as in their future veterinary and animal science careers, including in their places of work. To date, one DVM class has graduated with an increased awareness of the importance of CC and ways to apply it, and many

J. Gongora (✉)
Sydney School of Veterinary Science; Indigenous Strategy and Services, Faculty of Science, The University of Sydney, Sydney, NSW, Australia
e-mail: Jaime.Gongora@sydney.edu.au

M. Vost
Education Portfolio, Faculty of Science, The University of Sydney, Sydney, NSW, Australia

S. Zaki · S. Sutherland · R. Taylor
Sydney School of Veterinary Science, The University of Sydney, Sydney, NSW, Australia

63

J. Frawley et al. (eds.), *Transforming Lives and Systems*,
SpringerBriefs in Education, https://doi.org/10.1007/978-981-15-5351-6_6

students have expressed that they see the relevance of CC in the curriculum and to their future careers.

Keywords Cultural competence · Veterinary · Professional practice · Culture · Diversity

The Importance of Cultural Competence

There is a growing national and international recognition of the importance of cultural competence and capacity in education, professional practice and community work and its role in helping to facilitate development of relationships and creation of opportunities to work collaboratively and respectfully with groups from diverse cultural and linguistic backgrounds including First Nations Peoples (Bradley, Noonan, Nugent, & Scales, 2008, Universities Australia, 2011a, b). Aligning with this, international and local veterinary accrediting bodies and associations have recommended that cultural awareness, cultural competence and diversity competence should be incorporated as one of the core graduate qualities in veterinary education, and have developed a competency framework to guide their members in the endeavour to foster respect, and collaborate with and in culturally and socially diverse groups and environments to promote animal, human and environmental health and wellbeing (AVBC, 2016; Hodgson, Pelzer, & Inzana, 2013; Molgaard et al., 2018; NAVMEC, 2011).

The disciplines of health and medicine have developed foundational and best-practice approaches in cultural competence in professional practice (e.g., CARE, 2009; Goode, Harris Haywood, Wells, & Rhee, 2009; Kodjo, 2009; Kurtz & Adams, 2019; Sobo, 2009; Sobo & Loustaunau, 2010; Trudgen, 2000). This is also the case in One Health, when veterinarians are working in interdisciplinary environments and the following factors are also important: the human–animal–environment interface; understanding global issues; and community development (Kahn, Kaplan, Monath, & Steele, 2008; Maud, Blum, Short, & Goode, 2012; Zinsstag, Schellingm, Wyssm, & Mahamatm, 2005).

The 2016 Australian census highlights the richness and diversity of cultural and social groups which are the clients that veterinary students will be dealing with during their professional practice. Australia is a culturally, demographically and linguistically diverse country. This poses great challenges and opportunities for veterinarians, especially when Australia has the highest rate of pet ownership in the world (62% of households for ~24 million pets) (AMA, 2016). Here we describe and reflect on a journey we took to assist in servicing of these social realities that started in 2012 when we designed the rationale, learning outcomes, content and pedagogy to embed cultural competence into the curriculum of the combined Bachelor of Veterinary Biology (BVB) and Doctor of Veterinary Medicine (DVM) program at the Sydney School of Veterinary Science (SSVS).

Defining Cultural Competence in the Context of the Veterinary Programme at Sydney School of Veterinary Science

Cultural competence was the major focus of the current work, and it was defined as a graduate quality for the BVB and DVM programmes as follows: *On graduation students will confidently and competently be able to demonstrate an understanding of the manner in which culture and belief systems impact delivery of veterinary medical care while recognising and appropriately addressing biases in themselves, in others and in the process of delivering their professional practices.*

Elements of cultural humility (commitment to self-assessment to manage and reduce the power imbalances in the practitioner–client interface: Tervalon & Murray-García, 1998), intercultural competence (capacity to work productively and positively within professional, working and educational environments of diverse cultures and perspectives: Gurin, Dey, Hurtado, & Gurin, 2002; Lee et al., 2018) and multicultural competence (ability to work with and interact with others who are culturally different from oneself in meaningful ways: Chun & Evans, 2016; Pope, Reynolds, & Mueller, 2004), were also embedded into pedagogy and curriculum content.

Cultural Competence in the Veterinary Curriculum

Through a consultation process (meetings and workshops) that occurred during the design phase for the BVB and DVM programmes over two years, including Indigenous peoples and centres for cultural competence and benchmarking with other veterinary schools, we identified some guiding principles for our approach. These include making learning outcomes evident and assessable across the degree programme, focusing on a curriculum that is relevant and linked to the veterinary profession. Other principles include embedding cultural competence vertically across the programme in existing units that we thought suitable to presentation of the curriculum content in a way that demonstrates the relevance of the material for the veterinary profession. Thus, we designed a roadmap of learning outcomes, which correspond to 24 sessions of face-to-face teaching, tutorials and practicals and various pieces of independent work across seven units of study. Teaching of cultural awareness in particular about Indigenous cultures started in the pre-veterinary units of study while cultural competence and other levels of cultural capacity were further developed through years 1 to 3 of the DVM, so students were equipped with knowledge, skills and resources to prepare for their intramural and extramural, clinical and non-clinical, rotations that take place mainly in year 4 of the DVM programme.

We framed and mapped the learning outcomes in a progressive way. Specifically, we take students through cognitive and affective domains (Bloom, 1956; Krathwohl & Anderson, 2009; Lynch, Russell, Evans, & Sutterer, 2009; O'Neill & Murphy, 2010) when understanding principles of cultural competence, their application to approaching real and simulated case scenarios underlined by reflections on the impact of the human–animal bond, and unconscious biases on interactions with clients and communities across cultural settings.

After considering a range of potential pedagogical approaches, we agreed that using a repertoire of teaching and learning methods would suit the multicultural and diverse international and local student cohort of the BVB and DVM programmes. We supported a vision for the teaching of cultural competence so that the skills, behaviours and values developed in students are considered to go deeper than only outcomes related to awareness of concepts.

Through diverse pedagogical approaches (Brockbank & McGill, 2007; Gewurtz, Coman, Dhillon, Jung, & Solomon, 2016; Kapur, 2008; Roselli, 1999; Strijbos & Fischer, 2007; Solomon, 2005; Sugerman, Doherty, & Garvey, 2000), we facilitated and fostered transformational learning to give students the opportunity to make a major shift in their perspective on the world, including in relation to areas like gender, race and class. We also supported students to take a critical perspective on the dominant culture. We approached curriculum content by following an adapted cultural competence continuum from cultural awareness, cultural knowledge, cultural sensitivity to cultural competence (Cross, Bazron, Dennis, & Isaacs, 1989, 2012; Chun & Evans, 2016; Farrelly & Lumby, 2009; Kiefer et al., 2013). We also enhanced understanding about the concept of cultural competence by introducing other dimensions and elements of cultural capacity such as diversity competence, cultural responsiveness, cultural humility, intercultural competence and multicultural competence (Abermann & Gehrke, 2016; Alvarez, Gilles, Lygo-Baker, & Chun, 2019; Bennet et al., 2004; Bennett, 2004; Bennett & Bennett, 2004; Brown, Thompson, Vroegindewey, & Pappaioanou 2006; Gallardo, Johnson, Parham, & Carter, 2009; Ippolito, 2007; Tervalon & Murray-García, 1998; Wagner & Brown, 2002) as illustrated (Fig. 6.1).

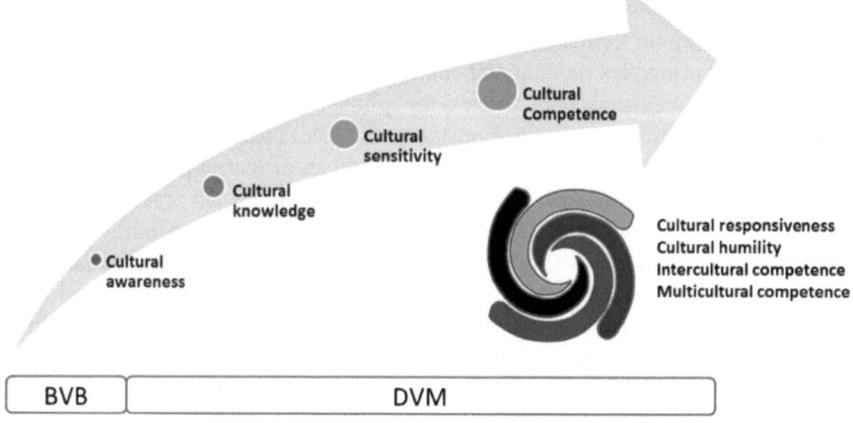

Fig. 6.1 Curriculum flow and cultural diversity dimensions used to implement the current work in the BVB and DVM programmes. The spiral denotes the dynamic interactions and movements of the different stages and dimensions of cultural competence and of cultural capacity

Highlights of the Implementation

Pre-veterinary Bachelor of Veterinary Biology Units of Study

The units of study topics included use of animals across cultures, non-human kin relationships in Indigenous cultures, Indigenous practices and knowledges in conservation and management of biodiversity, and weather knowledge related to animals (Green, Billy, & Tapim, 2010; Hart, 2010; Kutay, Mooney, Riley, & Howard-Wagner, 2012; Moller, Berkes, Lyver, & Kislalioglu, 2004). Various methods were used including co-teaching with Indigenous knowledge holders and development of or use of publicly available resources under the guidance of these knowledge holders. Students had the opportunity to engage with smoking ceremonies, cultural performances and workshops related to the presence and significance of animals in Indigenous dance, songs, paintings and storytelling.

Doctor of Veterinary Medicine

Cultural competence was introduced to DVM students as part of a One Health field trip activity in a local parkland frequented by humans, dogs, horses and wildlife. Students rotated through five learning stations focussing on: animal health; animal management; infectious diseases; zoonoses; and the impact of cultural competence and bias on the profession. This work is further described in Mor et al. (2018). Subsequently, we engaged students in individual and group reflections on their own and others' perceptions of animals and the significance of this when interacting with clients, with use of pre-recorded talks by people from diverse cultural heritages. Students were engaged in learning principles of culture, cultural diversity and cultural competence with a particular emphasis on unconscious and conscious biases and stereotypes and strategies to manage these.

Students were engaged in a class reflection on potential questions about the benefits of veterinarians learning about effective communication in cross-cultural environments. The focus was on principles of culturally effective communication across cultural environments and social groups as well as strategies to deal with tensions in cross-cultural environments (Adams, 2009; Bonvicini & Keller, 2006; Kodjo, 2009; Kurtz, 2006; Shaw, 2006). Students were also engaged in strategies related to the practice of active listening, types of questions and communication strategies in cross-cultural settings.

Teaching was structured to give students the opportunity to work through case studies based on experiences of practitioners and students during overseas placements and a space for self-reflection on conscious and unconscious biases and power-imbalance between practitioner and client, and ways of managing these challenges. To provide a context for cultural competence, one case study focused on shelter practice, veterinary euthanasia and cultural influences in Bangkok, Thailand.

Cultural competence was integrated within the topic of Animal Management Systems. Case studies on animal husbandry and management in rural and remote Australia and overseas were used to reflect on cultural competence opportunities and challenges. This included management of a conservation programme, and animal health in remote Australian Indigenous communities.

The pedagogy and curriculum content was one of the most complex in the DVM programme. It focused on the relevance and practice of cultural competence in research practice (Papadopoulos & Lees, 2002; Shalowitz et al., 2009) and community-based work and included all of the cultural capacity aspects described in previous units, but developed further. Students were introduced to the general aspects of the ethical and working guidelines (Queensland Health, 2015; NHMRC, 2018; RACGP, 2012) and history of dispossession, trauma, sorry business, gender roles, non-human kinship relationships and ethical guidelines when undertaking research in Indigenous communities by using the University of Sydney's Aboriginal Kinship Module and the Aboriginal Sydney Massive Open Online Courses.

Discussion

We have embedded diverse dimensions of cultural capacity, with an emphasis on cultural competence and some elements of intercultural competence and cultural humility, into pedagogy and content in seven units of study across the BVB and DVM programmes in the SSVS. This vertical integration of principles of theory and practice into veterinary curriculum addresses some of the recommendations by the international and local accreditation and association bodies for veterinary education (AVBC, 2016; Hodgson et al., 2013; Molgaard et al., 2018; NAVMEC, 2011). This work is a practical example of how to develop important non-technical skills in BVB/DVM students and graduates, so they are in a better position to engage effectively and respectfully with the global and local context of their professional practice, including in animal conservation, program management and community development (Brown et al., 2006; Graham, Turk, McDermott, & Brown, 2013; Kiefer et al., 2013; Shaw, 2006; Wagner & Brown, 2002).

The approach adopted was to introduce students to fundamental levels related to awareness which was scaffolded onto more complex levels of cultural competence and humility. The ultimate aim is to enhance students' ability to reflect on the impact of cultural belief systems present in themselves and in those they interact with during their professional practice across different cultural environments, diverse social groups and within intercultural settings. Furthermore, this work provided opportunities for students to increase awareness of the historical context of dispossession, exclusion, inequity and injustice towards minorities and underrepresented groups such as Aboriginal peoples, and how this has generated intergenerational trauma (e.g., Atkinson, 2013; Brice, 2004; Bobba, 2019) that needs to be considered in professional practice. This awareness and the incorporation of some Indigenous perspectives as well as the contribution to a better climate and environment that celebrates and recognises Indigenous cultures is a first step towards decolonising (Harvey & Russell-Mundine, 2019) the veterinary curriculum.

The current work has contributed to the implementation of the principles recommended by Universities Australia (2011a, b) by enhancing the cultural capacity of veterinary students and developing a more inclusive veterinary curriculum that celebrates and recognises the contributions and cultures of Aboriginal and Torres Strait Islander peoples. We consider that this curriculum work is also having a positive influence in fostering inclusive classroom environments for the retention of and satisfactory achievement by Indigenous students (Drysdale, Chesters, & Faulkner, 2006; Oliver, Rochecouste, & Grote, 2013). The SSVS has also influenced cultural change across the University of Sydney as it has been considered one of the best practice examples for the integration of CC into curriculum. We found that when the University of Sydney established cultural competence as one of the graduate qualities for all academic programmes and developed a rubric to assess this, there was significant alignment of requirements with what we had developed for the BVB and DVM programmes since 2012.

Conclusions

We have enhanced cultural capacity in veterinary students by integrating cultural competence vertically into curriculum and developing contextual learning activities with increasing sophistication to align with students' interests and to progress them along the cultural competence continuum. This work has contributed to a trend of positive change in behaviours and attitudes in veterinary students to give them foundational skills in cultural competence to effectively and respectfully interact within multicultural and diverse social environments. To achieve this, we have introduced students to the cultural competence concept, allowing them to identify the challenges when working in cross-cultural environments, develop strategies and then implement them through repetition, reinforcement and reflection.

Acknowledgments The offices of the Deputy Vice-Chancellor Indigenous Strategy and Services, and Education, University of Sydney, have supported this work financially through Indigenous compacts and grants. We would also like to acknowledge the valuable advice given during interactions with Dr Gabrielle Russell from the University of Sydney's National Centre for Cultural Competence and A/Prof Tawara D. Goode from Georgetown University's National Center for Cultural Competence.

References

Abermann, G., & Gehrke, I. (2016) The Multicultural classroom—a guaranteed intercultural learning space? *Research Forum at the Austrian University of Applied Sciences 2016* (S. 1–7), Wien.

Alvarez, E. E., Gilles, W. K, Lygo-Baker, S., & Chun. R. (2019). Teaching cultural humility and implicit bias to veterinary medical students: a review and recommendation for best practices. *Journal of Veterinary Medical Education*, 1–6. https://doi.org/10.3138/jvme.1117-173r1.

Animal Medicines Australia. (2016). *Pet Ownership in Australia*. Barton ACT.

Atkinson, J. (2013). *Trauma-informed services and trauma-specific care for Indigenous Australian children*. Resource sheet no. 21 produced for the Closing the Gap Clearinghouse. Australian Institute of Health and Welfare.

Australasian Veterinary Boards Council. (2016). Accreditation standards Version 5.

Bennett, J. M., & Bennett, M. J. (2004). *Developing intercultural sensitivity. an integrative approach to global and domestic diversity*. In: DaLandis, J. Bennett, & M. Bennett (Eds.) *Handbook of Intercultural Training*, 3rd Edition. (pp. 147–165). Thousand Oaks: Sage.

Bennett, M. J. (2004). Becoming interculturally competent. In J. S. Wurzel (Ed.), *Toward multiculturalism: A reader in multicultural education* (2nd ed., pp. 62–77). Newton, MA: Intercultural Resource Corporation.

Bloom, B. S. (1956). *Taxonomy of educational objectives*. Vol. 1: Cognitive domain. New York: McKay, pp. 20–24.

Bobba, S. (2019). Ethics of medical research in Aboriginal and Torres Strait Islander populations. *Australian Journal of Primary Health*. https://doi.org/10.1071/PY18049.

Bonvicini, K., & Keller, V. F. (2006). Academic faculty development: the art and practice of effective communication in veterinary medicine. *Journal of Veterinary Medical Education, 33*(1), 50–57.

Bradley, D., Noonan, P., Nugent, H., & Scales, B. (2008). Review of Australian higher education: Final report. Available from https://vital.voced.edu.au/vital/access/services/Download/ngv:32134/SOURCE2.

Brice, G. (2004). A way through? Measuring Aboriginal mental health/social and emotional well-being: community and post-colonial perspectives on population inquiry methods and strategy development. Monograph. Canberra: National Aboriginal Community Controlled Health Organisation Inc.

Brockbank, A., & McGill, I. (2007). *Facilitating reflective learning in higher education*. Buckingham: Society for Research into Higher Education and Open University Press.

Brown, C., Thompson, S., Vroegindewey, G., & Pappaioanou, M. (2006). The global veterinarian: The why? The what? The how? *Journal of Veterinary Medical Education, 33*(3), 411–415.

CARE: Community Alliance for Research and Engagement. (2009). *Principles and guidelines for community university research partnerships*. CARE Ethical Principles of Engagement Committee: Yele Center for Clinical Investigation.

Chun, E., & Evans, A. (2016). The politics of cultural competence in higher education in: Rethinking cultural competence in higher education: An ecological framework or student development.

Cross, T. L., Bazron, B. J., Dennis, K. W., & Isaacs, M. R. (1989). *Towards a culturally competent system of care: A monograph on effective services for minority children who are severely emotionally disturbed*. Washington, DC: CASSP Technical Assistance Center.

Cross, T. L. (2012). Cultural competence continuum. *Journal of Child and Youth Care Work, 24,* 83–85.

Drysdale, M. M., Chesters, J. E., & Faulkner, S. (2010). Footprints forwards: Better strategies for the recruitment, retention and support of Indigenous medical students. In A. Larson, & D. Lyle (Eds.), *A bright future for rural health: Evidence-based policy and practice in rural and remote Australian health care* (pp. 26–30). Australian Rural Health Education Network.

Farrelly, T., & Lumby, B. (2009). A best practice approach to cultural competence training. *Aboriginal and Islander Health Worker Journal, 33*(5), 14–22.

Gallardo, M. E., Johnson, J., Parham, T. A., & Carter, J. A. (2009). Ethics and multiculturalism: Advancing cultural and clinical responsiveness. *Professional Psychology: Research and Practice, 40*(5), 425–435. https://doi.org/10.1037/a0016871.

Gewurtz, R. E., Coman, L., Dhillon, S., Jung, B., & Solomon, P. (2016). Problem-based learning and theories of teaching and learning in health professional education. *Journal of Perspectives in Applied Academic Practice, 4*(1), 59–70. https://doi.org/10.14297/jpaap.v4i1.194.

Goode, T., Harris Haywood, S., Wells, N., & Rhee, K. (2009). Family-centered, culturally, and linguistically competent carte: essential components of the medical home. *Pediatric Annals, 38*(9), 505–512. https://doi.org/10.3928/00904481-20090820-04.

Graham, T. W., Turk, J., McDermott, J., & Brown, C. (2013). Preparing veterinarians for work in resource-poor settings. *Journal of Veterinary Medical Education, 243*(11), 1523–1528. https://doi.org/10.2460/javma.243.11.1523.

Green, D., Billy, J., & Tapim, A. (2010). Indigenous Australians' knowledge of weather and climate. *Climatic Change, 100*(2), 337–354.

Gurin, P., Dey, E. L., Hurtado, S., & Gurin, G. (2002). Diversity and higher education: Theory and impact on educational outcomes. *Harvard Educational Review Home, 72*(3), 330–367. https://doi.org/10.17763/haer.72.3.01151786u134n051.

Hart, M. A. (2010). Indigenous worldviews, knowledge, and research: The development of an indigenous research paradigm. *Journal of Indigenous Voices in Social Work, 1*(1), 1–16.

Harvey, A., & Russell-Mundine, G. (2019). Decolonising the curriculum: Using graduate qualities to embed Indigenous knowledges at the academic cultural interface. *Teaching in Higher Education, 24*(6), 789–808. https://doi.org/10.1080/13562517.2018.1508131.

Hodgson, J. L., Pelzer, J. M., & Inzana, K. D. (2013). Beyond NAVMEC: Competency-based veterinary education and assessment of the professional competencies. *Journal of Veterinary Medical Education, 40*(2), 102–118. https://doi.org/10.3138/jvme.1012-092R.

Ippolito, K. (2007). Promoting intercultural learning in a multicultural university: Ideals and realities. *International Journal of Educational Research, 12*(5–6), 749–763. https://doi.org/10.1080/13562510701596356.

Kahn, L. H., Kaplan, B., Monath, T. P., & Steele, J. H. (2008). Teaching "one medicine, one health". *American Journal of Medicine, 121*(3), 169–170. https://doi.org/10.1016/j.amjmed.2007.09.023.

Kapur, M. (2008). Productive failure. *Cognition and Instruction, 26*(3), 379–425. https://doi.org/10.1080/07370000802212669.

Kiefer, V., Grogan, K. B., Chatfield, J., Glaesemann, J., Hill, W., Hollowell, B., ... & Urday, K. (2013). Cultural competence in veterinary practice. *Journal of the American Veterinary Medical Association, 243*(3), 326–328.

Kodjo, C. (2009). Cultural competence in clinician communication. *Pediatric Review, 30*(2), 57–64. https://doi.org/10.1542/pir.30-2-57.

Krathwohl, D. R., & Anderson, L. W. (2009). *A taxonomy for learning, teaching, and assessing: A revision of Bloom's taxonomy of educational objectives.* Longman.

Kurtz, S. (2006). Teaching and learning communication in veterinary medicine. *Journal of Veterinary Medical Education, 33*(1), 11–19.

Kurtz, S. M., & Adams, C. L. (2009). Essential education in communication skills and cultural sensitivities for global public health in an evolving veterinary world. *Revue Scientifique et Technique, 28*(2), 635–647.

Kutay, C., Mooney, J., Riley, L., & Howard-Wagner, D. (2012). Experiencing Indigenous Knowledge online as a community narrative. *The Australian Journal of Indigenous Education., 41*(1), 47–59. https://doi.org/10.1017/jie.2012.8.

Lee, A., Poch, R., Smith, A., Kellym, M. D., & Leopold, H. (2018). Intercultural pedagogy: A Faculty Learning Cohort. *Education Sciences, 8*(4), 177. https://doi.org/10.3390/educsci8040177.

Lynch, D. R., Russell, J. S., Evans, J. C., & Sutterer, K. G. (2009). Beyond the cognitive: the affective domain, values, and the achievement of the vision. *Journal of Professional Issues in Engineering Education and Practice, 135*(1), 47–56.

Maud, J., Blum, N., Short, N., & Goode N. (2012) *Veterinary students as global citizens: exploring opportunities for embedding the global dimension in the undergraduate veterinary curriculum.* (DERC research papers 32). Royal Veterinary College and Development Education Research Centre, Institute of Education.

Molgaard, L. K., Hodgson, J. L., Bok, H. G. J., Chaney, K. P., Ilkiw, J. E., Matthew, S. M., et al. (2018). *Competency-based veterinary education: Part 1—CBVE Framework.* Washington, DC: Association of American Veterinary Medical Colleges.

Moller, H., Berkes, F., Lyver, P. O. B., & Kislalioglu, M. (2004). Combining science and traditional ecological knowledge: monitoring populations for co-management. *Ecology and Society, 9*(3), 2.

Mor, S., Norris, J., Bosward, K., Toribio, J., Ward, M., Gongora, J., et al. (2018). One health in our backyard: Design and evaluation of an experiential learning experience for veterinary medical students. *One Health, 5,* 57–64. https://doi.org/10.1016/j.onehlt.2018.05.001.

NMHMR: National Health and Medical Research Council. (2018). *Ethical conduct in research with Aboriginal and Torres Strait Islander Peoples and communities: Guidelines for researchers and stakeholders.* Commonwealth of Australia: Canberra.

North American Veterinary Medical Education Consortium (NAVMEC). *Roadmap for Veterinary Medical Education in the 21st Century.* Report and recommendations. 2011.

O'Neill, G., & Murphy, F. (2010). *Guide to taxonomies of learning.* UCD Teaching & Learning. Available from http://www.ucd.ie/t4cms/UCDTLA0034.pdf.

Oliver, R., Rochecouste, J., & Grote, E. (2013). *The transition of Aboriginal and Torres Strait Islander students into higher education.* Sydney, NSW: Office of Learning and Teaching. Department of Education. Australian Government. Available from https://ltr.edu.au/resources/SI11_2137_Oliver_Report_2013.pdf.

Papadopoulos, I., & Lees, S. (2002). Developing culturally competent researchers. *Journal of Advanced Nursing, 37*(3), 258–264.

Pope, R., Reynolds, A. L., & Mueller, J. A. (2004). *Multicultural competence in student affairs.* San Francisco, CA: Jossey-Bass.

Queensland Health. (2015). *Sad News, Sorry Business: Guidelines for caring for Aboriginal and Torres Strait Islander people through death and dying.* State of Queensland (version 2). Available from http://healthbulletin.org.au/articles/sad-news-sorry-business-guidelines-for-caring-for-aboriginal-and-torres-strait-islander-people-through-death-and-dying/.

RACGP: Royal Australian College of General Practitioners (2012)- *An introduction to Aboriginal and Torres Strait Islander health cultural protocols and perspectives.* South Melbourne, Victoria.

Roselli, N. (1999). El mejoramiento de la interacción sociocognitiva mediante el desarrollo experimental de la cooperación auténtica. *Interdisciplinaria, 16*(2), 123–151.

Shalowitz, M. U., Isacco, A., Barquin, N., Clark-Kauffman, E., Delger, P., Nelson, D., et al. (2009). Community-based participatory research: A review of the literature with strategies for community engagement. *Journal of Developmental and Behavioral Pediatrics, 30*(4), 351–361. https://doi.org/10.1097/DBP.0b013e3181b0ef14.

Shaw, J. R. (2006) Four core communication skills of highly effective practitioners. Veterinary clinics of North America. *Small Animal Practice, 36*(2), 385–396.

Sobo, E., & Loustaunau, M. (2010). *The cultural context of health, illness and medicine.* 2nd ed. Santa Barbara, CA: Praeger. Sobo, E. (2009). *Culture and meaning in health services research: an applied anthropological approach.* Walnut Creek, CA: Left Coast Press; 2009.

Solomon, P. (2005). Problem-based learning: A review of current issues relevant to physiotherapy education. *Physiotherapy Theory and Practice, 21*(1), 37–49.

Strijbos, J., & Fischer, F. (2007). Methodological challenges for collaborative learning research. *Learning and Instruction, 17*(4), 389–393.

Sugerman, D. A., Doherty, K. L., & Garvey, D. E. (2000). *Reflective learning: theory and practice.* Dubuque, IA: Kendall/Hunt Publishing Co.

Lee, A., Poch, R., Shaw, M., & Williams, R. D. (2012). Engaging diversity in undergraduate classrooms–a pedagogy for developing intercultural competence. *ASHE Higher Education Report, 38*(2), 1–132.

Tervalon, M., & Murray-García, J. (1998). Cultural humility versus cultural competence: A critical distinction in defining physician training outcomes in multicultural education. *Journal of Health Care for the Poor and Underserved, 9*(2), 117–125.

Trudgen, R. (2000). *Why warriors lie down and die: towards an understanding of why the Aboriginal people of Arnhem Land face the greatest crisis in health and education since European contact.* Darwin: Aboriginal Resource & Development Services.

Universities Australia. (2011a). *Guiding Principles for Developing Indigenous Cultural Competency in Australian Universities*, October, DEEWR, 1–32. Canberra.

Universities Australia. (2011b). *National best practice framework for indigenous cultural competency in Australian universities*, October, DEEWR, 1–422. Canberra.

Wagner, G. G., & Brown, C. C. (2002). Global veterinary leadership. Veterinary Clinics of North America. *Food Animal Practice, 18*(3), 389–99. https://doi.org/10.1016/s0749-0720(02)00034-8.

Zinsstag, J., Schellingm, E., Wyssm, K., & Mahamatm, M. B. (2005). Potential of cooperation between human and animal health to strengthen health systems. *Lancet, 366*(9503), 2142–2145. https://doi.org/10.1016/S0140-6736(05)67731-8.

Chapter 7
Progressing STEM Education Using Adaptive, Responsive Techniques to Support and Motivate Students

Collin Grant Phillips and Fu Ken Ly

Abstract The components of a series of workshops in science, technology, engineering and mathematics (STEM) for Indigenous school students, conducted by the Mathematics Learning Centre (MLC) in conjunction with the Faculty of Engineering and Information Technologies at the University of Sydney (UoS), are described. The MLC has developed and taught the mathematics component of these STEM workshops in 2017. This chapter builds on Phillips and Ly (2020). The STEM workshops have been developed using a distinctive, innovative approach that has drawn on the experience, knowledge and philosophy of the MLC, as well as the key pillar concepts of cultural competence, advanced by the National Centre for Cultural Competence at the UoS. How these concepts have been progressed to the principle of cultural plasticity is discussed in the context of the MLC and the STEM workshops. Our approach has been to give the students a genuine voice in their own learning experience and is encapsulated in the themes of 'knowing' and 'responding'. These themes and their connections to cultural competence and cultural plasticity are discussed. We also describe how these themes have been employed. Input is encouraged from the students through surveys before, interactions during and feedback after the workshops. How this feedback has been used to evolve, progress and improve the workshops over the three-year period is then described. In particular, the students have identified interest in some motivational topics as well as a desire to explore certain mathematics topics from school. The principles of knowing and responding are demonstrated in both the inclusion of motivational topics, and subsequently, the evolution of these (along with other) topics through continuous improvements from the students' input. This evolution is outlined in the context of the motivational topic of *Codes and Code Cracking*. This has been used to explore advanced ideas and concepts in the mathematical realm that may be beyond the students' current experience. The response of the students to the STEM workshops and the use of the programme more widely is also described. Throughout the article we provide reflections on our experience with the workshops in the light of offering insights that may be used as a resource for future initiatives.

C. G. Phillips (✉) · F. Ken Ly
Mathematics Learning Centre, The University of Sydney, Sydney, NSW, Australia
e-mail: collin.phillips@sydney.edu.au

© The Author(s) 2020
J. Frawley et al. (eds.), *Transforming Lives and Systems*,
SpringerBriefs in Education, https://doi.org/10.1007/978-981-15-5351-6_7

Keywords Mathematics education · Indigenous education · STEM education · Cultural plasticity

Introduction

Some of the key pillar concepts of cultural competence have been at the heart of the philosophy of the Mathematics Learning Centre (MLC) at the University of Sydney (UoS) from its inception in 1984. Because there is no obligation for students to attend the MLC to satisfy any part of any course at the UoS, the MLC must be adaptive to individual needs and perspectives, responsive to changing modes of learning, receptive to a broad spectrum of cultural worldviews and inputs, and culturally responsive, for any student to continue engaging with the MLC.

The National Centre for Cultural Competence (NCCC) at the UoS has informed and advanced the use of cultural competence in the MLC. Both the pre-existing philosophy of the MLC and the work of the NCCC have been instrumental in developing and improving a workshop programme to engage, improve and motivate Indigenous participation in science, technology, engineering and mathematics (STEM) at the UoS. The MLC joined the Faculty of Engineering and Information Technologies (FEIT) at the UoS to provide the mathematics component of these STEM workshops in 2017. Throughout this chapter we refer to the mathematics component of the STEM workshops as the workshops for brevity. These STEM workshops are run as week-long intensive programmes for Indigenous school students from across Australia. The details of the first year of the programme are presented in Phillips and Ly (2020). The current work reports on the progress, evaluation and evolution of the workshop programme.

In this work we outline how the philosophy of the MLC and the pillar-concepts of 'perspective', 'worldview' and 'resilience', as outlined and developed by the NCCC, have contributed to the development of the workshops. For us the philosophy and pillar-concepts of the NCCC and MLC intersect at key principles. These include the importance of the perspective of the individual, knowing the student worldview and responding in a way that addresses the student's individual resilience and ensures they can feel safe and supported.

Distinctively, we recognise that STEM may have its own cultural elements and that in the process of learning STEM an amalgamation/blending of cultures can take place. Consequently, it has been necessary to expand upon the key pillars of cultural competence to consider or allow for this possible amalgamation in our own approaches and attitudes to teaching. We shall refer to this quality as cultural plasticity, which is defined as being receptive to, learning from and adapting to the cultural perspectives of others (Phillips & Ly, 2020).

In contrast, *cultural rigidity* is the inability or refusal to be receptive to, learn from, or adapt to the cultural perspectives of others. An individual can certainly exhibit cultural plasticity, but this can also be adopted by a group or be a quality of an environment. The details of this concept, and how it has affected our interactions with students will be expanded upon through this work.

Implementing and Fostering Cultural Competence

In this section we demonstrate how key concepts of cultural competence have affected, informed and been fostered at the MLC and the workshops. In particular, we discuss the concepts of the perspective, worldview and resilience.

Individual Perspective and Worldview

> Every one of us is born into a particular time, place, social context and culture. In fact, we see everything through the filters of our culture and experiences; and our ideas, views, opinions and behaviours are not 'objective' and independent... (NCCC Cultural Competence Module 1.2, Journey of Self-discovery: Worldview)

The MLC has supported a culturally diverse student cohort from its inception including the support of Indigenous students. The MLC was established in 1984 (the first such initiative in Australia) and from its outset has supported students of educationally, socially and culturally diverse backgrounds. Thus, at the MLC we recognise that 'people bring different ways of knowing, being and doing' (Excerpt from NCCC Module 4, Know your world, See my world.). Consequently, the principle of being responsive to an individual's perspective and worldview has been at the core of the MLC from the outset. This can be emphasised by the fact that many, if not most, of the students of the MLC would have tried the mainstream forms of learning and found them insufficient. Often this is because some of the conventions, norms, values, pre-suppositions, language and ideas of the conventional mathematics classroom or learning channel may not align well with their own perspectives. For example, a student may, for whatever reason, find it difficult to appreciate how a presented solution is the 'best' solution, yet is able to arrive at a solution using an approach that from their viewpoint may be more natural and plausible. What is 'best' can be contingent on attributes such as 'succinctness', 'beauty', 'rigour', 'insight', 'elegance' which are, arguably, cultural elements of the discipline. Indeed, even what constitutes a 'proof' in mathematics has evolved over the centuries. It is important that such viewpoints not be disparaged or dismissed. Even for practising mathematicians, it is generally acknowledged that there is a diversity in perspectives, which is not only accepted but recognised as fruitful for the discipline. For example, some researchers may prefer a visual-spatial approach to their work, while others prefer the so-called 'analytic' approach. These differences in approach are part of what Burton (2009) calls a 'heterogeneity' in research practice. It has often been the case that a new perspective has transformed the discipline.

Thus, at its core, to operate effectively the MLC must be culturally respectful, responsive, resilient and agile. Since participation in our services is completely voluntary, the fact that students continue to return to the MLC is strong evidence for the effective implementation of cultural competence. We attempt to accommodate, respond to and support different perspectives at the MLC through two interrelated themes. First, we seek to *know the student* by acknowledging that, 'at the heart of any culturally responsive teaching programme is a genuine knowledge of the students and their needs', albeit recognising that this knowledge is 'often determined by the worldview held by the teachers' (Perso, 2012, p. 30). Secondly, we also acknowledge that:

> culturally responsive teachers *respond* to the cultural knowledge, prior experiences and performance of students to make learning more appropriate and effective for them. They teach to and through the strengths of their students, reducing the discontinuity between the home cultures of these students and the social interaction patterns of the classroom (Boon & Lewthwaite, 2015, p. 456; paraphrasing Gay, 2000).

In this sense we also attempt to *respond appropriately.*

Knowing and Responding at the Mathematics Learning Centre

> Recognising that people bring different ways of knowing, being and doing is important if we are to find ways to include culturally informed ways of learning and working together (NCCC Cultural Competence Module 4; Know your world. See my world.)

Knowing and responding play important roles in cultural competence, since developing an awareness of how you and others around you perceive the world can have a crucial impact on your interactions. Our experience in knowing and responding in the context of the MLC is outlined below. We begin to know the student during our enrolment process. This includes an informal interview followed by the student completing a short enrolment form. Here we seek to gather information about the student such as any past mathematics courses, where and when they have studied mathematics, the degree in which they are currently enrolled and why they think they need our help. The students have the opportunity to provide any cultural information at this stage, however, this is completely voluntary.

Even though the information gathered during the enrolment process is valuable, interactions in the classroom are the principal means of knowing and responding to our students. These include observing each of the student's individual modes of learning, how each student interacts with other students and our interactions with each student. Knowing the student informs how we respond. By considering their experience and background, we may tailor and design explanations or examples for each individual student that are different to those available in their standard courses.

Here we give examples of how some of the MLC students' prior experiences can inform our teaching. Some students identify that they have missed a section of mathematics because of being sick, moving schools or some other circumstances beyond their control. Many have also cited having a 'bad' teacher as the crucial factor. Past teachers could make them feel inadequate or even stupid with comments like, 'you should know this', 'this is trivial' or even just using words such as 'easy', 'obvious' or 'simple' to describe new mathematical ideas. In these contexts, students can conclude that they could not ask the questions they needed to for fear they would be regarded as 'stupid questions'. Past and current learning environments could also have had a negative impact. For instance, many of our students feel that in the past there was little opportunity for them to have input into their learning in teacher-led classes or in group learning modes when other students dominated discussions. All these factors can contribute to the accumulation of gaps in their mathematical understanding and knowledge. Moreover, many students at the MLC feel there is little opportunity in the mainstream classes to learn or shore-up foundational concepts, and because mathematics builds on past concepts, perhaps more than any other subject, this inability to shore-up foundations leads to more unstable learning that compounds or exacerbates any anxiety towards mathematics they already feel.

These are just some of the ways that past experiences can affect present mathematical learning and, although not obvious, these experiences and perspectives can be intimately linked with culture. Different students from different backgrounds will have different perspectives of what is appropriate behaviour in different learning circumstances. Thus, learning environments will affect each student differently. There are increasing discussions in the literature on the cultural and social structures embedded in the teaching and practice of mathematics (Aslan Tutak, Bondy, & Adams 2011; Averill et al., 2009; Burton, 2009).

Knowing all this, our response is to try to provide a safe, non-confrontational, environment where students feel they can share their past experiences. Many of our first contact sessions with students involve just listening to a student's past experiences, associations and even traumas in learning mathematics. Often this may help the student to dismantle some of these past anxieties or traumas. This process can be transformative.

> Sometimes using words like "this should be easy" or "obviously this follows this" can make you feel as if there's something wrong with you since it wasn't "easy" or "obvious" for you,. ... It can feed into other insecurities that you might have about your ability, whether you belong there etc. The biggest difference with the MLC was that I felt the tutors were empathetic in their teaching style and were patient enough to understand what it felt like to me to not get it. (communication from past MLC student).

One of the main operating principles of the MLC is that there are no stupid questions. This means we will help with foundational concepts, going as far back as necessary. As one past student comments about the MLC: 'It was extremely healing for me and I felt safe in that space to ask questions that I normally would be ashamed to ask in a lecture'.

Another operating principle is that rather than just referring the student to a *standard approach*, we first attempt to understand a student's approach in solving a problem or understanding concepts. This is another way of 'knowing' the student. We can then respond by attempting to work on the problem together by using their 'tools' of thinking. This cooperative process can highlight mistakes, uncover misconceptions or even (delightedly) reveal a completely new solution method. Importantly, it also provides a way for the student to reconcile their individual thought processes and perspectives with standard approaches. There is a growing body of literature on principles of good practice in mathematics support that the interested reader may consult (e.g., Croft et al. (2011). These principles of knowing and responding have significantly informed our teaching in the workshops.

Knowing and Responding in the Context of the Workshops

In approaching the workshops, and with respect to the themes of knowing and responding, it was considered vital to:

- remain aware that cultural perspectives are individualised and that each person (course coordinators included) perceives their reality through their own unique cultural perspective; and
- provide a means whereby the students can provide feedback about their background and perspectives.

Additionally, by inviting feedback from the students we were able to demonstrate our interest in the backgrounds of the students and indicate that we wanted to provide a responsive and supportive learning and teaching environment. Thus, as the first step we asked the Faculty of Engineering and Information Technologies to survey the students about their home state and what level of mathematics (if any) the students were studying at school. The course designers considered it critical to provide an avenue for students to have an input into the mathematics workshop. We also thought it is important to understand the different dimensions of the students. Not only was it important to know the students' backgrounds, but also what the students thought they needed help with, as well as their understanding, confidence and interests. For this reason, to gain a better understanding of their needs, wants and perspectives, each of the students (in the first two years of the workshops) was asked to respond to a survey. The survey asked the students to identify the topic in mathematics that they thought may be most useful or interesting. Some topics were listed as options, but they could nominate any topics they liked. The students were asked to rate the difficulty of a mathematical question to get an insight into their mathematical backgrounds. The students were also asked to gauge their overall confidence in mathematics. All of these details were used to design the workshops. Details of this survey process (including results) are given in Phillips and Ly (2020).

Perhaps most importantly, the process of inviting the students for their input and then using this input to design the workshops and interactions throughout the workshops indicates to the students that their input is not only welcome but is valued in the learning and teaching process. In this way the key elements of 'receptiveness', 'learning from' and 'adaptation' of cultural plasticity have resulted in the students' roles in the workshops evolving from just being recipients of knowledge to being active participants and evolving further to being co-conveners or co-producers of their own learning.

Resilience

> Resilience... is the ability to go through something and then start to recover. Cultural competence requires people to build resilience... Very importantly, by developing your cultural competence you will be less likely to harm people who are perhaps less resilient or have had more trauma than you have by being culturally insensitive (NCCC Cultural Competence Module 1.3, Journey of Self-discovery: Resilience).

One of the chief aims of the MLC is to build student confidence in their mathematical abilities and this can be critical to a student's progress in their studies. The process of studying mathematics often involves facing disappointments, setbacks, failures, dead-ends, mistakes, and trying again (perhaps with a different approach or different perspective). Thus, in the first instance, we observe a link between confidence and resilience (in mathematics).

Secondly, sensitivity and responding carefully to those with lower confidence (or resilience) in mathematics is one of the core principles of the MLC. The authors estimate that approximately fifty percent of the students seeking first time help at the MLC may harbour concerns, fears or even trauma associated with prior engagements with mathematics. Many of this cohort have sought the support of the MLC specifically because within the standard learning channels there may be little help or acknowledgement available of past or present fears of the mathematical sciences. At the MLC it is critical to acknowledge and remain receptive to such trauma. For instance, for some of our students who are stressed or even traumatised, the worst first approach would be to try to teach mathematics or statistics without talking about past troubling experiences. Often, we need to allay fears and possibly address past trauma before engaging in any learning material. MLC teachers are knowledgeable about referring students to counselling services, and often students, after experiencing the support of the MLC, will volunteer that they have subsequently sought counselling or disability services.

Relentlessly, and possibly unconsciously, demanding a student face mathematics before addressing their fears and concerns can increase and compound fear and trauma for the students. This principle has also been pivotal in our approach to the STEM workshops. Our research into the workshop students' backgrounds revealed that their previous school studies ranged from Year 9 to Year 12 from schools across Australia. For this reason, and from the individual pre-workshop surveys, the teachers of the mathematics component of the workshop decided that there should be two separate curriculum streams for the topics of *Algebra* and *Calculus*. This way pre-calculus students (predominantly from Years 9 and 10) could opt into the *Algebra* stream, whereas students at a more advanced level (predominantly from Years 11 and

12), could choose to engage with the concepts and practices of differential calculus, albeit at an introductory level.

For us, *insisting* that a Year 9 student attend a workshop session that required a further two years of mathematical study of calculus is unacceptable. The course coordinators wanted to avoid at all costs any such student surmising, incorrectly, that they were not 'good enough' to continue with mathematics or even that university or STEM was not for them. To provide only one form of curriculum support for these students would have been insensitive and incompetent on our part and quite possibly produced harm or even trauma.

Fostering Cultural Competence Amongst Students

The learning environment of the MLC is one that is conducive to developing and growing student cultural competence. First, students of different ages, cohorts, backgrounds, cultures and worldviews, who may not otherwise interact with one another (either by choice or by lack of opportunity) come together at the MLC to work and support each another in a community. At the MLC the students (and, of course, the teachers) are continually exposed to different perspectives, worldviews and different approaches to learning, as well as different approaches to mathematical problems. Such different approaches can cultivate a receptiveness to other perspectives, encourage self-reflection and thereby foster cultural competence. Secondly, the support and encouragement of the students' peers and the teachers at the MLC can mean the difference between giving up or trying again. As students consistently engage and re-engage with their learning, their confidence (resilience) can grow, which could have an impact on not only their performance but other areas of their lives. Thus, the environment of the MLC provides ample opportunity for students to develop and grow in cultural competence.

The Need for Cultural Plasticity in Teaching and Learning

> Culture is the learned and shared knowledge that specific groups use to generate their behaviour and interpret their experience of the world. It is a defining and vital aspect of every human being. Every culture has its own standpoint or worldview that informs our ways of thinking, and how we behave and act. (NCCC Cultural Competence Module 1.2, Journey of Self-discovery: Worldview)... each discipline has its own knowledge system as well the knowledge systems that individuals bring to their studies and workplace (NCCC Cultural Competence Module 4; Know your world. See my world.)

It has been contended that learning mathematics at times necessitates conceptual changes, or perspectival shifts to make progress (Breen & O'Shea, 2016; Cobern, 1996). Some familiar examples may include the concepts of functions, limits and costs and quotient groups, as discussed in Breen and O'Shea (2016). Since mathematics provides one way of looking at, organising, and thinking about reality—if not explicitly, then perhaps implicitly through the fact that so many other disciplines draw upon mathematics—it is conceivable that this shift can affect one's worldview, whether consciously or unconsciously, for better or worse. Indeed, words associated with threshold concepts in the literature include transformative, troublesome, irreversible, which seems to indicate a more profound effect on a person than a mere acquisition of knowledge. Thus, while educators often require and desire their students to undergo such conceptual changes it is worth noting that the process can be empowering but also possibly uncomfortable and difficult for the student, depending on their own worldview and identity.

It is also often recognised that there are cultural elements associated with mathematics. In her interviews with a group of mathematicians, Burton (2009) has identified some cultural elements of mathematics and classifies these elements into either the mathematical culture which is 'the environment in which the mathematics is encountered and learned and inevitably influences the culture of mathematics' (Burton, 2009), or the culture of mathematics, by which she means:

> those aspects of mathematics that are recognisably discipline-related (such as the particular attitudes towards beauty, rigour, structure, etc.). Learning the importance of these aspects of the culture of mathematics is part of induction into the mathematics community of practice.

To the latter we could perhaps add attributes that could be associated with science more generally, such as reproducibility, refutability, proceeding from a set of axioms or postulates, internal consistency, and even being receptive to a new concept unless and until it is disproven.

Whilst students need to embrace new concepts and ideas as part of the process of learning mathematics, we also wish to recognise that the student may also need to navigate (and perhaps absorb) an array of, perhaps unspoken, cultural elements associated with the discipline. For instance, the concept of a limit may have associated notions of rigour and succinctness that we are expecting students to assimilate implicitly, if not explicitly. Furthermore, although students can merely tolerate or endure mathematics, mathematical educators often rightly or wrongly, consciously or unconsciously, desire their students to embrace, engage and perhaps adopt some of the worldview and cultural aspects of the discipline into their own lives. In effect then, we are asking for a sense of 'plasticity' in the students, that is, an 'open-ness' on their part to the expanding and embracing of new perspectives. The term 'culture acquisition' has been sometimes adopted (Aikenhead, 1996), but we prefer the sense of open-ness to change that 'plasticity' suggests. However, we suggest that sometimes such cultural elements can be their own barrier and that a kind of plasticity on the part of the educators themselves, and thus of the classroom as a whole, can be productive and reduce barriers.

Here we offer a few examples of how this may occur in the context of mathematical teaching and learning. Students often bring different ways of approaching their work, for example in organising, writing, thinking and speaking. A student may prefer to use certain symbols or may present a calculation in a long sequence of steps that may be 'inelegant'. For the purposes of instruction and at least in that learning environment, it could be productive to adopt the students' approach and attempt to operate and teach within the students' world. Thus, awareness of one's own cultural perspectives and a willingness to embrace the students' perspective may be needed. In essence, as much as possible, we are seeking to ensure that we ourselves are not barriers to our own message, and that as much as possible the students can engage with the discipline on its own merit. It is worth recognising at this point that science has itself been through such a plasticising process: 'Western science itself has gone through a process of philosophical and methodological evolution in which some of the underlying principles have given rise to different visions of scientific knowledge' (Pomeroy, 1994, p.65). This is as a result of having embraced and adopted perspectives and elements of different cultures and worldviews from around the world throughout time.

To appreciate how we have employed cultural plasticity in our teaching and learning contexts, it is important to understand the central role that the individual plays in each of those contexts, and it is this aspect that we turn to next.

The Role of the Individual and Cultural Plasticity

As we have alluded to earlier, responding appropriately to the individual needs of a student is an important aspect of the MLC. Here we discuss how this view is reflected in the literature. For many of the students, who seek the help of mathematics support centres, the standard Materials and methods of delivery have not adequately worked for them. This is largely because such material and its delivery are primarily designed for the 'traditional student', that is, those students entering tertiary education with a certain level of school education straight from schooling in the local system, who may also be from an assumed 'traditional' background. However, the broadening of participation of students with non-traditional backgrounds entering university has resulted in a 'much greater diversity of numeracy, mathematical skills and knowledge backgrounds across tertiary cohorts' (MacGillivray, 2008, p. 13). Consequently, a one-size-fits-all approach is becoming less appropriate and there is an increasing pressure to provide more diverse teaching material, lesson delivery and modes of learning, as well as an increased need for extra-curricular mathematics support.

Indeed, the literature on mathematics support recommends good practice as providing a tailored, individual, 'person-centered' approach (Croft, 2011; Delderfield et al., 2018). This is summarised well by Patel (2011) in her study of the effectiveness of various approaches to mathematics support:

> The individual occupies a key position in mathematics support since the student's very specific mathematical skills needs are addressed (Samuels & Patel, 2010). Situating the individual at the heart of learning is desirable as learning theories have highlighted. (Patel, 2011, p. 15)

Likewise, the importance of individuality occupies an important part of culturally responsive pedagogy for Indigenous students. It is recognised that:

> one approach to culturally responsive pedagogy that works with one Aboriginal student may not necessarily work with another (Krakouer, 2015). Consequently, any framework for culturally responsive pedagogy with Aboriginal students' needs to consider the individuality that rests within all students as well as within and between Aboriginal language groups. (Daniels-Mayes, 2016, p. 53)

Indeed, Perso (2003, 2012) in her discussion of pedagogy for Indigenous school children—whilst recommending useful behaviours and practices for the classroom—nonetheless observes that:

> If over-generalizations are made about the preferred learning styles of Indigenous and minority children, there is a risk of stereotyping. What can result is a biased pedagogy that may result in the needs of some children not being addressed through the pedagogies used. Just as there are many Indigenous cultures, so there are many Indigenous learning styles (Perso, 2012, p. 51)

She advocates that to be effective in such contexts, teachers need to 'learn and know' about, and 'respond' to each individual student. It is now generally recognised in the literature that knowing and responding to the individual are important components of any culturally responsive pedagogy (Paige, Hattam, Rigney, Osborne, & Morrison, 2016).

The above discussion reinforces our perspective that the role of the individual is critical in all of the spheres in which the MLC operates. In the STEM workshops this is further accentuated by a number of factors. First, the students in the workshops travelled from different states across Australia and thus belong to different Indigenous communities. Furthermore, the students are of different ages, have had varying levels of, quality of, and even access to, education, and also have different mathematical backgrounds. This wide diversity only reinforced the importance of maintaining the needs of the individual at the core of the workshops. Whilst we could have concluded that it is too difficult to accommodate the 'sheer diversity' of our students, we thought that the small class sizes meant that we should try to respond to each individual student's perspective. We did this by inviting feedback and allowing each student a voice throughout the workshop. In the process, personal viewpoints about STEM were considered, the teachers could also re-evaluate and possibly become aware of their own pre-suppositions in their instruction (and readjust their approach if needed). Furthermore, any common (cultural) elements amongst the group can be picked up and the class can be adapted around this element.

'Knowing' and 'responding' to the individual, therefore, is how we have employed cultural plasticity and in the next section we discuss how such principles informed and improved the motivational cryptography sessions.

Cultural Plasticity in the Cryptography Sessions

In this section we aim to demonstrate how we have employed cultural plasticity in the workshops, specifically through the themes of knowing and responding to the individual. To this end we outline how we have responded to the individual input and perspectives of the students in the motivational sessions on *Codes and Code Cracking*, and how these sessions have been shaped by their input.

First, cryptography is not a core topic of the HSC curriculum in most states of Australia. Prior to the workshops in 2017 and 2018 we asked the students through a questionnaire, 'What mathematical topics do you think would be most useful or interesting?'. While there was no restriction on the topics the students could nominate, to encourage responses, the topic of *Codes and Code Cracking* was included as one of the suggestions. This topic was consistently nominated in the top two topics along with HSC curriculum-based topics such as Algebra and Differentiation. For this reason, and from the feedback of the students during and after each of the workshops, the cryptography sessions have formed a major component of the workshops.

The process of seeking and acting on the feedback from the students demonstrates a genuine attempt for us to know and respond to the students. Rather than pre-supposing what an (Indigenous) school student may, or may not, be interested in, we allowed each individual student to speak for themselves. We believe this also established from the outset a cultural element of listening, learning and adapting to student feedback.

Knowing and responding continued throughout the workshops and impacted the modes of learning and how the core concepts of cryptography were conveyed. The modes of learning evolved considerably, both during and from one workshop to the next. For example, the students responded enthusiastically to discussion about where codes have been used, and it was clear from the first workshop that the students were very interested in how cryptography played a significant part in World War II. Indeed, some of the students already knew about details of the German 'Enigma' machine and its flaws. In response to this enthusiasm and prior knowledge, these discussions were increased at each subsequent workshop and even incorporated a short YouTube clip from *Flaw in the Enigma Code* (Grimes, 2013).

We note that this prior interest and knowledge is resonant with the fact that 'high-performing' Indigenous students tend to report higher levels of engagement with out-of-school STEM activities (in comparison with all Indigenous and non-Indigenous students) as some have observed (McConney, Oliver, Woods-McConney, & Schibeci, 2011; Woods-McConney & McConney, 2014). Although such a prior interest (as a common cultural element amongst the group) could be surmised from the programme selection process, it is important to note that we did not assume this would be true for all the students, choosing rather instead to let the students indicate and express their individual enthusiasm and prior engagement in person. As another example, in the Rubik's cube motivational sessions in 2017, some of the students surprised us by demonstrating a facility in 'solving' the Rubik's cube prior to attending our sessions.

We responded by encouraging these students to participate in the teaching through sharing their expertise, as well as leading and supporting their peers.

How the sessions engaged with the core concepts of cryptography also evolved through responding to student input. We decided to adopt the Vigenère cypher method, since we felt this method could demonstrate the core concepts of cryptography effectively and appropriately. In its simplest form, encoding and decoding a message using this method involves shifting letters by a pre-determined shift. To encode a message with a '*1*-key' of 'shift k', each letter in the message is replaced by a letter that is k places along the alphabet, with the convention that A is the next letter after Z. For example, for a '*1*-key' Vigenère cypher of 'shift 3' then the 'message' *HAL* is encoded as *IBM*.

Originally, we asked the students to encode a message by shifting the letters of a message along the alphabet and then decoding the resultant code by shifting the letters in the code 'backwards' to recover the message. We responded to the enthusiasm of the students by incorporating a Socratic exchange with questions such as, 'If you were given a code that was encoded by shifting the letters in the original message by a fixed shift, how would you try to guess the shift and then crack the code'? To promote thought about how to do this, a histogram of 'standard' English text (Appendix 1) was also given to the students. Subsequently, the discussions concluded that to decode a message we could find the most frequent letter in the code and compare this to the most frequent letter in the English language (being the letter e), and or produce a 'graph' of the letters in the code and compare this with the histogram of 'standard' English text (as given).

Another example is how we might increase the difficulty of decrypting a message. Originally, we simply explained the concepts of a multi-key cypher to the students and asked them to crack a code using this method and the shifts that we gave them. However, after observations and feedback from the students it was decided that we should ask the students: 'If you can crack a 1-key code by using the histogram approach, and guess the (single) shift, how could we make a message harder to crack'? The students readily answered that we could use different shifts on different parts of the message. The discussion then continued that using different shifts on different parts would 'blur' the distribution of letters in the code, so it will look different to the standard English distribution.

This way of demonstrating the concepts using a Socratic exchange with the students allowed them not only to 'discover' the concepts themselves (and thus 'adopt' or take ownership of the concepts), but to express it in their own perspective. In particular, if their responses did not include discussions around producing a graph, then that would have told us something about their perspective on the topic, and we would have had to modify the subsequent activities accordingly. Other improvements we have made in response to the input of the students include a redesign of the set of exercises. For details see Appendix 2.

The examples above illustrate the two-way process of learning and growing (by teachers and students alike) through knowing and responding. In this regard the cultural growth of both the students and the teachers is facilitated and improved by exploring together the new techniques, concepts and culture of the mathematics.

We would like conclude with the following observation: in each workshop (as in the cryptography section) participation evolved to the point where students, teachers and 'house-parents'—volunteers who accompanied the students through all of the STEM workshop programme—adopted 'cooperation over competition with a preference for cooperative and collaborative learning' (Boon & Lewthwaite, 2015; Duchesne, McMaugh, Bochner, & Krause, 2015). In this sense, the group adopted a learning model embracing cultural plasticity. Thus, cultural plasticity can be embodied not just in individuals, but within a learning environment.

Summary of Survey Results from the Workshops

Here we provide a summary of the survey results across the three-year period from 2017 to 2019, with a more detailed analysis of the 2017 results in Phillips and Ly (2020).

The students were asked to rate whether and how their understanding of the subjects taught in the workshop (curriculum and motivational topics combined) had changed (Table 7.1). The Faculty of Engineering and Information Technologies (FEIT) also asked the students to rate the different components of the whole STEM workshop programme using a five-point Likert scale. The students' satisfaction with the mathematics component of the workshop are as follows: 2017, 63/70; 2018, 42/55; 2019, 29/40. These ratings were particularly high and ranked in the top few topics covered in the whole workshop programme for every year of the STEM workshops.

The conveners of the workshop also conveyed to the authors that the students were very happy with the mathematics part of the workshop and that their understanding and confidence in mathematics and STEM as a whole had grown as a result of the whole workshop programme. The results are particularly encouraging given that students will see, learn and even embrace very new ideas and concepts in learning mathematics and as such can find mathematics and even the mathematics component of STEM an exacting and even challenging experience at times. We note, however, that students can find mathematics challenging and even confronting due to a number of different reasons beyond learning new concepts as outlined in this work.

To discover how the perceived increase in understanding differed between the curriculum and motivational topics, in 2018 and 2019 the students were further asked

Table 7.1 Student ratings of whether and how their overall understanding of the mathematics taught in the whole workshop had changed for the three years 2017, 2018 and 2019. The ratings were for a five-point Likert scale: 1 decreased a lot; 2 decreased; 3 stayed the same; 4 increased; 5 increased a lot

2017	2018	2019
100% increased or increased a lot	82% increased or increased a lot, the rest stayed the same	88% increased or increased a lot, the rest stayed the same

Table 7.2 Students were asked to rate whether and how their understanding of the Algebra or Calculus (curriculum) and Coding or Polytope (motivational) topics taught in the workshop had changed. The ratings were on a five-point Likert scale as in Table 7.1

	2018	2019
Curriculum Topics Algebra or Calculus	73% increased or increased a lot, the rest stayed the same	78% increased or increased a lot, the rest stayed the same
Motivational Topics Coding or Polytope	91% increased or increased a lot, the rest stayed the same	100% increased or increased a lot, the rest stayed the same

to rate how their understanding had changed in the curriculum and motivational topics separately. This was to discover whether and how the students' perceived increase in understanding differed between the curriculum topics and motivational topics (Table 7.2). Across the three years, the understanding in mathematics generally stayed the same or increased, with the majority rating their understanding as having increased in some manner. In comparing curriculum with motivational topics (across 2018 and 2019) we see that the perceived understanding in motivational topics increased slightly more.

The students were also given the opportunity to offer open-ended comments. Generally, the students wanted more time in the sessions, in particular the motivational activities. They also highlighted the usefulness and value of the curriculum topics. On the other hand (in 2018 and 2019), while they thought motivational topics were interesting and engaging, they were less certain about their value or usefulness for their future.

Finally, while the students enjoyed and gave positive feedback for all the sessions, it is worth noting that the reasons for the students' enjoyment of the curriculum topics may differ from the motivational topics. For the curriculum stream the students highlighted value and usefulness, while for the motivational stream the students highlighted engagement and interest.

Embedding Cultural Competence More Widely

The MLC has supported a culturally diverse student cohort from its inception including the support of Indigenous students. The MLC was established in 1984 (the first such initiative in Australia) and from its outset has supported students of educationally, socioeconomically and culturally diverse backgrounds. As described earlier in the chapter, the environment of the MLC has provided and continues to provide ample opportunity for students to develop and grow in cultural competence.

The STEM workshops have contributed to further embedding cultural competence across several dimensions. The first is the impact on the student participants, many of whom have continued to higher education in STEM degrees with some enrolling in the FEIT at the University. The post surveys revealed a strong motivation to engage and embrace STEM subjects. In addition to the recorded uptake of further STEM study, we regard the growth in the students' confidence and curiosity in exploring STEM as part of their lives as one aspect of their growth in cultural competence.

Related to this is the impact on and personal growth of the teachers involved. The experience of facilitating the workshop has contributed to a widening of the perspectives of the teachers and a deep appreciation of the individual perspectives as well as the capacity and potential of the students. For example, one of the teachers commented, 'I was surprised how quickly the students knew each other, formed subgroups and how quickly the class warmed up as the workshops went on'. Perhaps this positive theme to the workshop may be appreciated in light of the observation from Boon and Lewthwaite (2015, p. 456, paraphrasing Duchesne et al., 2015) that Aboriginal cultures 'emphasise relationship over task and cooperation over competition with a preference for cooperative and collaborative learning models in classrooms'.

Another dimension includes further initiatives for Indigenous students at the UoS. The contribution of the nominees to workshops has been highly regarded by the FEIT and the mathematics component has grown with each workshop. In addition, the MLC has continued to support Indigenous students in their STEM studies at the University, some of whom may have been past STEM workshop participants.

Furthermore, Dr. Phillips attended a NCCC Cultural Competence Leadership Programme, and is also now a panel member for the development of the University of Sydney's *Indigenous Strategy and Services* foundation year for Aboriginal and Torres Strait Islander students, in particular the STEM component. The experiences gained from the STEM workshops can be invaluable for all such initiatives.

Fourthly, the dissemination of the results and experiences more widely at conferences and in publications can contribute to the embedding of cultural competence more broadly. For instance, the evaluation methods employed the concepts of knowing and responding as well as the desire to provide students with a genuine voice. If adopted, these methods can serve to provide avenues and environments where cultural competence and, perhaps, cultural plasticity can grow and develop.

Conclusions

Learning mathematics can present more of a challenge than any other subject, because the ideas and concepts can seem, at least at first, more different than any other form of thinking. In order to learn new mathematical concepts, we need to expand our worldview to understand, encapsulate, incorporate and even adopt these ideas into our cultural perspective. However, all new ideas will be understood through our own perspective and perhaps draw upon our own cultural competencies. To abstract these new ideas and concepts to larger overarching mathematical concepts will require us to enter further into the mathematical realm where we may be able to draw less and less on our cultural references for help.

Furthermore, culture plays a deeper and often unrecognised role in our learning. The manner in which a subject is taught is often exclusively from the cultural perspective of the teachers and course designers. Giving students mathematics texts, presenting the mathematics in a pre-determined format, requiring the students then to answer specific exam questions about the material in a fixed time and environment, grading the responses, and classifying all of the dimensions of understanding using a single metric, is the product of a particular worldview. This perspective can have the effect of disenfranchising students from different backgrounds. We should acknowledge the culture that is embedded in an educational system and even a subject. Acknowledging the important part that worldview, perspective, resilience, culture and cultural competence play in the learning process can allow us to use cultural competence to enhance and improve understanding.

In this chapter we suggest that to learn new ideas (in mathematics), students are asked to grow and even adopt new cultural perspectives. In this sense, students are asked to go beyond acknowledging that there are alternate worldviews, but to understand and even adopt some of these ideas and extend their culture in the process. To do so requires not only cultural competence, but a form of cultural growth and plasticity. We further suggest that, as our experience with the MLC and the STEM workshops has shown us, it can be productive if we as teachers are equally as receptive to adopting some of the students' (cultural) perspectives. This is at least consistent with our expectations that students understand our ideas, concepts, perspectives and indeed culture. We are not suggesting that this is always possible to achieve, but the willingness to try can itself open up new perspectives and new ways of working and learning together.

At the MLC and the workshops, we have sought to cultivate this sense of cultural plasticity through attempting to know and respond to student needs continuously and in ways that are appropriate for each individual.

Acknowledgments The authors wish to express their gratitude to their teachers Erwin Lobo, George Papadopoulos, Alexander Majchrowski and Collin Zheng. Also they wish to acknowledge the dedication and partnership of our colleagues from the FEIT: Keiran Passmore, Christina Bacciella, Alberta-Mari Nortje and Petr Mateus, as well as the work and support of Gabrielle Russell, Juanita Sherwood and the rest of the NCCC. The authors wish to thank Jackie Nicholas, Sue Gordon and the people of Academic Enrichment at the UoS for their years of support and dedication.

Appendix 1

See Fig. 7.1.

Appendix 2

The teachers of the workshops responded to the students valued and continual feedback by dedicating much time and effort to improving details. Examples of this can

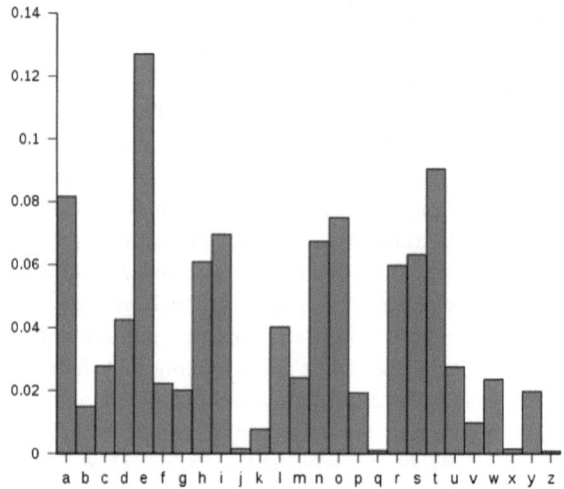

be found in the continual improvement of the questions asked in the cryptography
session of the workshops as shown in Fig. 7.2.

As an example, to make the process of cracking a 2-key Vigenère code less time-
consuming, so that more emphasis could be placed on the code cracking process and
less on the mechanics, Question 2 was progressively improved as follows:

- The letters in the code were coloured to simplify the process of picking out which
  parts of the code should be shifted by different amounts.
- Different groups were tasked with, focussing on either the odd or even letters and
  collaborating with other groups once they had decrypted their subset in order to
  recover the entire message.

Vigenère Ciphers Tuesday 9th of July 2019

1. Make up a short message. Then by shifting each letter in the
    message by 4 letters encode your message. Then pass the code to a
    second group to decode. Maximum length is one sentence. The 1-
    letter key for this shift is ...

2. The following has been enciphered using a 2-letter key. See if you
    can find the key and decode the message!

Hint: It is a weather forecast.

```
WIAKOGMWNQUBOMTWYVPVNUHQUTFQUBOMDMZBSQNPAEPV
KAIMJWTQUOUWYBOMYTFNPNAMLVAWLQNPAMLVRQSWTMAZ
LAWMYPVCYQUBOMTQKLSMVNAPLLHGAPLVIMJWTQUOSQNP
AQUBOMLDLVPVNYBMZBPWUBOZLMLVJZFXAQVVRMFQZUSK
```

Fig. 7.2 First (of three) pages of the Vigenère Cipher project sheets. The second question gives
the first code that needs 'cracking'

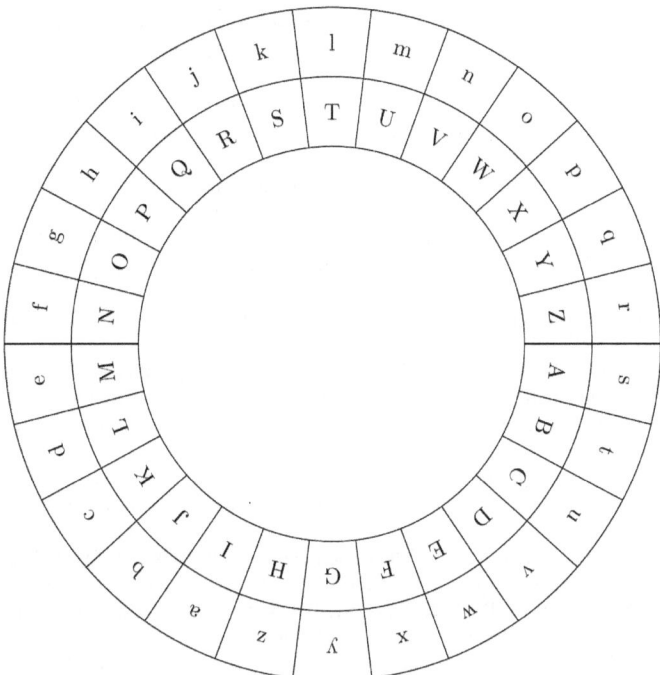

Fig. 7.3 Representation of an Alphabet Wheel. This graphic was distributed to the students to assist with cracking the code in the question. The shift in the illustration is 8, which is used for the even letters in Question 2 (of Fig. 7.2)

- The message was specifically designed and modified so that the most common letter in each subset (odd or even) was e, ensuring that it is simpler to guess the correct shift in the first instance.
- Alphabet wheels were given to the students, as shown in Fig. 7.3 to reduce the time spent on the mechanistic aspects of shifting the (sections) of the code.
- The value of these and other improvements, which are somewhat hidden in subsequent workshops, becomes apparent as the students managed to cooperate and use their various cracked section to reconstruct the hidden message, as well as enthusiastically crack quite complex codes, in their own time.

References

Aikenhead, G. S. (1996). Science education: Border crossing into the subculture of science. *Studies in Science Education, 27,* 1–52.

Aslan Tutak, F., Bondy, E., & Adams, T. L. (2011). Critical pedagogy for critical mathematics education. *International Journal of Mathematical Education in Science and Technology, 42*(1), 65–74.

Averill, R., Anderson, D., Easton, H., Te Maro, P., Smith, D., & Hynds, A. (2009). Culturally responsive teaching of mathematics: Three models from linked studies. *Journal for Research in Mathematics Education, 40*(2), 157–186.

Boon, H. J., & Lewthwaite, B. E. (2015). Signatures of quality teaching for Indigenous students. Paper presented at the Australian Association of Research in Education (AARE), 29 Nov–2nd Dec, University of Notre Dame, Fremantle, Western Australia.

Breen, S., & O'Shea, A. (2016). Threshold concepts and undergraduate mathematics teaching. *PRIMUS, 26*(9), 837–847. https://doi.org/10.1080/10511970.2016.1191573.

Burton, L. (2009). The culture of mathematics and the mathematical culture. In O. Skovsmose, P. Valero, & O. R. Christensen (Eds.), *University science and mathematics education in transition*. Boston, MA: Springer.

Cobern, W. W. (1996). Worldview theory and conceptual change in science education. *Science Education, 80*, 579–610.

Croft, A. C., Gillard, J. W., Grove, M. J., Kyle, J., Owen, A., Samuels, P. C. & Wilson, R. H. (2011). Tutoring in a mathematics support centre: a guide for post-graduate students. Edgbaston: The National HE Stem Programme. Retrieved from http://www.mathcentre.ac.uk/resources/uploaded/46836-tutoring-in-msc-web.pdf.

Daniels-Mayes., S. M. (2016). *Culturally responsive pedagogies of success: Improving educational outcomes for Australian Aboriginal students* (Unpublished doctoral thesis), University of South Australia.

Delderfield, R. & McHattie, H. (2018). The person-centred approach in maths skills development: Examining a case of good practice. *Journal of Learning Development in Higher Education, 13*.

Duchesne, S., McMaugh, A., Bochner, S., & Krause, K. L. (2015). *Educational psychology: For learning and teaching*. Melbourne: Cengage Learning.

Gay, G. (2000). *Culturally responsive teaching: Theory, research, and practice*. New York: Teachers College Press.

Grimes, D. (2013). Flaw in the enigma code [Video file]. Retrieved from https://www.youtube.com/watch?v=V4V2bpZlqx8.

Krakouer, J. (2015). *Literature review relating to the current context and discourse on Indigenous cultural awareness in the teaching space: Critical pedagogies and improving Indigenous learning outcomes through cultural responsiveness*. Australian Council for Educational Research.

MacGillivray, H. (2008). Learning support in mathematics and statistics in Australian Universities. Australian Learning and Teaching Council Report. Retrieved from http://www.olt.gov.au/resources?text=MacGillivray+2008.

McConney, A., Oliver, M., Woods-McConney, A., & Schibeci, R. (2011). Bridging the Gap? A comparative, retrospective analysis of science literacy and interest in science for Indigenous and non-Indigenous Australian students. *International Journal of Science Education, 33*(14), 2017–2035.

National Centre for Cultural Competence. (2019). Journey of self-discovery: Worldview; Journey of self-discovery: Resilience; What do you mean by 'cultural competence'?; Know your world. See my world. Retrieved from https://sydney.edu.au/nccc/training-and-resources.html.

Paige, K., Hattam, R., Rigney, L., Osborne, S., & Morrison, A. (2016). *Strengthening Indigenous participation and practice in STEM: University Initiatives for equity and excellence*. Magill: University of South Australia.

Patel, C. (2011). *Approaches to studying and the effects of mathematics support on mathematical performance* (Unpublished PhD Thesis), Coventry University, UK.

Perso, T. (2003). *Improving Aboriginal numeracy: a book for education systems, school administrators, teachers and teacher educators*. Perth, Australia: Mathematics, Science & Technology Education Centre, Edith Cowan University.

Perso, T. (2012). *Cultural responsiveness and school education with particular focus on Australia's First Peoples: A review and synthesis of the literature*. Centre for Child Development and Education, Darwin, Northern Territory: Menzies School of Health Research.

Phillips C., & Ly F. K. (in press). Mathematics education for Indigenous students in preparation for engineering and information technologies. In N. Borwein, & J. Osborn (Eds.). *From analysis to visualization: A celebration of the life and legacy of Jonathan M. Borwein.* New York: Springer.

Pomeroy, D. (1994). Science education and cultural diversity: Mapping the field. *Studies in Science Education, 24,* 49–73.

Woods-McConney, A., & McConney, A. (2014). *Indigenous student success in science.* Perth: Murdoch University.